MADE 'EM CRY

GERRY BRENT

4x156 100gsm coated

MADE 'EM CRY

CRY

GERRY BRENT

First published in Great Britain in 2012 by The Derby Books Publishing Company Limited, 3 The Parker Centre, Derby, DE21 4SZ.

ISBN 978-1-78091-064-2

Printed and bound by Copytech (UK) Limited, Peterborough.

Dedicated to the memory of
George Herbert Ellis
and to his family – to whom I apologise if any of the
recollections contained in this come as any kind of unpleasant
surprise.

Georgie-Porgie pudding and pie
Kissed the girls and made 'em cry

From an 18th-century children's nursery rhyme supposedly reflecting
the intemperate behaviour of King George III or his son, later George IV.

The Belgians swear and curse
The French eat and drink
The British wash and shave
The Germans fight like devils
But when it comes to girls, they are all the same

Popular Belgian verse, spring 1915.

6

Acknowledgements

◇◇

It would not have been possible for me to trace and confirm details of George's activities without the assistance of fourteeneighteen/research of Leamington Spa, Karl Noble, Collections Officer of the York & Lancaster Regimental Museum at Rotherham Arts Centre and the British Newspaper Library at Colindale in North London. My thanks to all these.

I am also indebted to my close friend Dennis Tate who, although he hardly knew him, has always encouraged my interest in events connected to George Ellis, accompanied me on visits to the battlefields of Ypres and The Somme and many museums and who read and provided opinion on an earlier draft of this text. These are the sort of things a real friend does.

To Peter Cherry, another good friend, who helped me hone the text into something coherent by providing wise counsel.

that.

To Judy, my wife, for listening to the frustrations and excitement over the years as I attempted to gather information together and for her diligence when we visited the British Newspaper Library which allowed us to confirm George's stories concerning the farm workers' strike and his part in that.

Lastly to George's family who provided me with many memories, photographs and documents as well as encouragement to actually attempt to set this down.

INTRODUCTION

<<<<<<<<<<<<<<<<<<<<<<<<<<<<<<<<<<<<<<<<<<<<<<<<<<<<<

George Ellis was my Uncle – who married my mother's twin sister. He lived from 1899 until 1988.

He was a countryman from North Essex and spoke in a rich dialect typical of that region in East Anglia. I cannot recall his stories without hearing them in his voice. Therefore, wherever I attribute comments or stories to George in this text, I attempt to write these as he spoke them.

This needs a little explanation.

The first person singular 'I' – and other words phonetically similar (find, right, rifle, life, time, etc.) – always sounded like 'oi' as in 'oil'. That is how I show it throughout.

'Oi sh'ink so' ('I should think so') means that 'I agree with you' or 'Of course you should do that/do it like that'.

'Oi reckon' ('I reckon') has a similar meaning to 'Oi sh'ink so' but is less strongly affirmative.

9

This showed that he had some respect for them. I have no idea where the use of this expression comes from unless it is from the common French expression for 'mate' which is 'mon vieux'. My Dad also used this expression but it is less commonly heard nowadays.

It is also worth attempting to explain that the North Essex dialect has some common phonetic peculiarities. When wishing to be slightly or strongly assertive the end of sentences are spoken with a rising emphasis – I have always called it a sort of 'singing'. (Not to be confused with the Australian tone so frequently – and, to me, annoyingly – used today where each sentence is left 'hanging' with a query at the end of it.) George might have said 'Oi've never seen anyone so cross in all m'loif' ('I have never seen anyone so cross in all my life'). That would have been spoken as: (lower intonation) 'Oi've never see anyone so cross in…' (change to rising inflexion) '…all m'loif'.

Most of the attempts to represent the peculiarities of the North Essex dialect are, I hope, apparent to the reader because the context for George's comments are all obvious. At least I hope that to be the case.

Gerry Brent
Newton-by-Toft
Lincolnshire
2012

George Ellis pictured when home on leave in 1919. His York & Lancaster
Regimental shoulder flash can be seen.

11

CHAPTER ONE

<><><><><><><><><><><><><><><><><><><><><><><><><><><><><><><><><><><><><>

I had taken George out with me for the evening. As a, then, enthusiastic 'learner of my trade' I had got myself invited to look at a pig farmer's particular innovation and had got him to agree to me 'Bringing along my old uncle who is staying with us'. Although George was no pig specialist, he enjoyed looking at anything to do with agriculture having worked in it for most of his days. In fact, he seemed to really enjoy doing anything we suggested when he came to stay with us. A real easy going sort of bloke.

We stopped at a pub in a Lincolnshire village after our farm visit and the bar was empty when we entered. It was quite typical of pubs at that time – I'm talking of the mid-to-late 1960s. It was there to dispense beer and to provide a haven for its 'locals' – none of them were apparent at the point that we entered the pub though.

walls on two sides of the bar with about five of the tables scattered between them. The seats were hardly welcoming being, in places, torn padded leather covered strips held in place by brass-headed nails tacked around the edges to secure them to the wooden seats and the backs of these bench-like arrangements were hardboard with patterns formed into it by perforations. The walls above the seats may have been painted cream at some point – or perhaps had just faded to be that colour. The evening sunshine just about prevented the bar from appearing totally depressing.

George sat down while I went to the bar and waited for the landlord to appear – when he did so he looked at me and nodded with his eyebrows raised – his way of asking what I wanted. I ordered two pints of bitter – and a whisky for George.

When I turned round with the drinks George had rolled one of his quite dreadful fags, it rested on his lips and he was coaxing it into light with his old silver-framed lighter, highly polished with continual wear. I smiled at the total lack of welcome from the place and rehearsed my opinion of what we had seen on the farm that we had been to. George let me talk and occasionally gave me a 'Mm-hmm' or a 'Oi reckon' – his usual ways of agreeing with a statement.

He took a good mouthful of beer and a sip at his whisky – by now, I noticed his fag had begun to turn the usual sort of brown, and he began by saying 'Well, no oi-er…' – it should be explained that, whenever he introduced a new topic he either began with that preface or an alternative 'Well, yes oi-er…'

And then he began to talk breaking only to pass some money to me when I went to order a couple more pints and his whisky – these days I would not have drunk so much knowing that I had to drive us home.

13

to recount some of his memories but here he was voluntarily recounting an episode from his usually-closed memory bank. I just listened as he leaned back and said:

Well, no oi-er... 'course we had allus bin told never to volunteer so when they asked fer a detachment o' three oi stood dead still and was surprised when moi corporal took a smart step forrard and gave me a nudge as he went. With the two of us stepping out our mate did too and the sergeant told the three of us to report to the adjutant's office straightaway.

Oi asked the corp what the bloody hell he thought he was doin' dropping us in for somethin' – he smiled and said, that we'd soon foind out. 'Course he'd got wind that they needed messages and documents ter be taken ter Paris and that a detachment o' three was considered proper given the fact that some o' them blasted Jerry's were still a bit keen on taking pot shots at us an' that.

He was given rail warrants and details of where ter go and who ter hand over the documents bag to when we got to Paris and, 'though we'd smartened ourselves up for the parade we were told ter go and do it all again and ter report back in an hour before we set off so that we didn't let the Regiment down. When we did report we had a second big surprise of the morning – we were handed 10 francs each to cover our costs – a ruddy fortune as far as we were concerned – but it came with a warning that we had better be back in four days time or else... We also went to the paymaster fer our pay and marched to the station and troid to imagine what our journey would be loike and it gradually dawned that we had got ourselves two nights in Paris – yee-ah! Bloody Paris.

'Course the journey was awful, overnight propped up in the corridor of the train which kept stopping as it crossed from Germany, through Belgium then France and onto Paris – seemed ter last for ever

14

as soon as we cleared the station and set off to get the business bit of the trip out the way. They kept old corp' hangin' around a bit but then he came out, smiled and grabbed us by the shoulders and said 'Eat and then – the girls'.

Cor them gals were lovely boy – oi'd never known anything loik it. Best two noits of me loif up 'til then. D'you know they washed you with potassium permanganate before – and after!'

I leant back laughing – and not a little amazed that George had seen fit to tell me all this – with absolutely no prompting. Him who was always so reluctant to tell anyone anything about the war – up until then anyhow.

As I suggested we should head off home he looked at me and closed it all off by saying *'Still you don't want to take no notice 'o me – silly old bugger that oi am'.*

I thought 'Oh! no, George – there's no way that I shall forget that' – nor was I to forget the bits that he saw fit to recount to me later. Why did he tell me these things and not his daughters (and they, and I, are pretty sure not his wife either) nor his brothers (at least his last surviving brother, John, assured me so when I asked him)? Perhaps he just wanted to get some of it 'off his chest' as he aged – there are others who did just the same…

AND – what the devil was he doing in Germany in the first place – and what was this Regiment that he had mentioned? Gradually I learned more from him and have been able to piece together more about some of the, to me, incredible experiences of a perfectly ordinary country bloke –who turned out to be – like all those who suffered similar experiences in World War One – anything but 'ordinary'.

15

Chapter Two

◇◇

I was eight years old when a combination of acute asthma, a respiratory infection and February weather killed my mother. Modern drugs would have probably prevented her early death – and allowed her to cope with the cold even in our, as homes then were, non-centrally heated place. Only 'posh' folk had central heating then – the rest of us relied on extra layers of clothes and sat closer to our coal fires when cold.

It is only in later life that I realise how our mother dying young impacted on my life and my character. Because I had a doting older sister to care for me, and our Dad, I didn't really suffer emotionally at that young age. I was still loved and cared for – albeit without my Mum being around. I know now that 'that's life' and just don't see the point in analysing it any deeper than that and looking for hidden 'meanings'. Such self-torture just turns you neurotic and helps to keep psychoanalysts in business.

with others. Affected by what happens around you – you become – in other words – who (or what) you are – is my view for good (hopefully) or ill.

One of the major outcomes of Mum dying young was that her twin sister – my Auntie Beat(rice) – seemed to feel the need to help support my older sister, Peggy, and my Dad in bringing me up. This manifested itself in my spending most of the summer school holidays with her and her family. Often, over the next eight years, I would spend the Easter break with them too.

Mum and Auntie Beat were non-identical twins and elder sisters to my Uncle Joe. I was too young to realise this myself but can relate to the fact that not only did they not look alike but the characters of Flo(rence) and Beat were also very different. Auntie Beat was always neat, tidy, busy and concerned what her husband thought of her. Flo, my Mum, was, apparently, a crusader who would sooner take off and help a relative stranger than worry about her home or cleanliness or what time of day it was. A 'good Samaritan' she apparently was – yet I have no recollection of regret because of that – she was just different from her sister.

Auntie Beat lived in a house on a raised corner of a large arable field, up a short lane which passed another pair of houses, in Essex. Her two daughters – my lifelong cousins and friends – Jane and Gill were, like my sister, also older than me. I am perfectly relaxed about the fact that I am the youngest 'cousin' by some years and quite clearly what would be called nowadays 'a mistake' or 'surprise'! Cousin Jane had just started work as a GPO telephonist when I first went down to stay but Gilly was only about five years older than me so was still at (Colchester Girls High) school. She was a real outdoor type and very accomplished sportsperson – just the sort of girl that a boy of that age can relate to.

work together to have enough in buckets indoors during frosty weather – although even that didn't prevent ice forming on top of the buckets overnight even when placed inside the house during winter. All water was heated on paraffin stoves – as was food – for drinking and eating and in a wood-fuelled boiler – or copper – for washing and, weekly, bathing. The zinc bath normally hung against an outside wall and was brought into the scullery for us all to take our turn to bathe.

Electric lighting was installed soon after the end of the war (1945) but there was only one power point (used for the radio) in the house so hand cleaning was always used.

Despite these conditions, so alien to our society today, it was all I knew and I just loved it. I was able to run wild over acres of land – either with cousin Gill or, when she had had enough of this troublesome 'townie' male cousin, with any of the local lads who might also be congregating around one of two adjacent farm yards and who were also trying to amuse themselves during the long summer holidays.

Building 'dens' having mock fights as ubiquitous 'Cowboys and Indians' or 'British and Germans' were important parts of our days broken only by the time spent in the fields following the binder round and chasing rabbits as they bolted out from the decreasing area of corn and attempted to reach the hedgerows before we got to them. I was 10 by the time that I could run fast enough to bowl over a rabbit with my stick and returned the following summer fully expecting to feed Auntie's family with rabbit only to find that they had all gone! Myxomatosis – a viral disease introduced from Australia to try to stem the damage done to agricultural crops by rabbits – had reached Essex and wiped most out during my break at school in London. This meant a few years of unbroken den trailers then – as combine harvesters began to be used to separate grain from straw in one pass – I drove tractors collecting the grain from the combine and drove them to the farm when there were no public roads to be crossed. Still loving every minute I found returning to home in Chelsea a nuisance and imposition on what I really liked doing!

The house described – and farm that I used as a never-ending source of entertainment and pleasure – both came thanks to Auntie Beat's husband who worked on the farm and the house was his 'tied cottage'.

Of course – her husband was George.

CHAPTER THREE

◇◇

How to describe the George I knew as a boy? Firstly, not that I would have known the meaning of the word then, taciturn would be the first element of his character. Quiet-to-being-withdrawn most of the time at home – he would open up a fraction more at others.

Auntie Beat was not only quick and twitchy in her movements but spoke quickly too in a high-pitched Essex accent. Lunch – or as it was called, dinner – would be ready to serve as soon as George arrived home from his work. Beat would immediately set off recounting her morning, who she may have spoken to, what had happened when she picked whatever excellent vegetables she had served from the garden, why she had told me off for doing what she had warned me not to (usually a wet foot from the stream we were supposed not to play near) and so on. George would offer an occasional *'Mm-hmm'* by way of agreeing and

20

dinner/lunch she might have received two or three back.

So he was a man of few words in everyday situations. He was a sociable sort of chap as well though. With a pint in his hand – or when organising a game of beach cricket on a couple of occasions when we all went to Walton on the Naze by bus – he could be very much the leader and what I recall my Dad describing as 'A good old stick'.

On the farm, his workplace, he was more likely to talk but I always noted some of the other men on the farm treated him with a bit of what I would now call 'reserve'. Partly respect for his many abilities. Partly, too, because of what – he eventually admitted to me later in life – *'O' course oi was a cussed bugger when oi loiked'*. Even at work he spoke less than most of the others alongside whom he toiled.

His many abilities. On the farm it was George who stepped forward to make or adapt things – not really mechanical though. If something needed making then he was the man who did it. I remember him completely kitting-out an old cowshed – after the dairy herd had been sold – to accommodate a laying flock of hens complete with nesting boxes, feeders, perches and drinkers – all but the latter he made from scratch. He would always thatch the stacks to keep the weather out until the corn was thrashed. He, one year, made a huge number of timber tripods onto which peas were forked until they had dried out and could be thrashed. Everyone looked to George to undertake these sort of tasks.

Then – he was the local barber. The image of him now with cap pushed forward on his forehead, fag in the corner of his mouth when work finished on Saturday dinner times is still very clear. One of the men off the farm or another local – or me when I was there – would sit on a chair outside the back door of his house

It seems that scissors and a comb in men's hands has that effect – given my experience of barbers around the country! He cut his own hair too – I can't remember how he managed that except he used a mirror to guide him. He did let his granddaughter Sandie take over that responsibility in later life though.

Another example of his ability to improvise was when I lost the screw-in nozzle of a super plastic water pistol. It would have been in the early years of items being made from plastic – I reckon around 1950. I had bought it in 'town' on the Friday and by Sunday morning was grieving because I had unnecessarily unscrewed the nozzle and lost it – typical behaviour in 10 year olds! I was distraught at my stupidity especially as it really was a super pistol and I had been aggravating my two cousins with it with much success. Not only that I couldn't wait to get it back to show my mates in London as it really did look like that one that Dan Dare used to vaporise 'the Treens' with in The Eagle comic! – a 'must' for every boy of my age at that time. George just said 'Give it a'me' and went into his garden shed with it (he had built that himself too). I saw him cutting a piece from a raw potato – this was wedged into the hole. Then he dropped some solder over the outside of the potato bung and edge of the pistol and, before that could cool and harden, pushed a needle through it and the potato beneath. He filled it with water – squirted me thoroughly and said *There yer go yer daft young 'apperth'*. It worked for years quite happily after George's repair!

Not just taciturn and 'handy' he was tough. I think that his natural bloody-minded streak had been hardened by his experiences in World War One so, yes – he was mentally very tough and showed virtually no emotion that I can recall – other than satisfaction at a job well done and happiness when he

22

he was no giant – below medium height (actually his medical when he was called up in 1917 had him at 5ft 4in) and build but he could still carry and lift more than anyone else on the farm – for longer too! I can recall a few of the farm staff struggling to get an axle loosened on a farm trailer – somehow it had slipped so that it was no longer centrally located. They called George. He took hold of the sledgehammer and had knocked it back into the correct position with about five mighty swipes. He was not very big but boy – was he powerful…

His toughness. Just as the Victoria plums and raspberries were ready in the garden this would always herald a plague of wasps appearing every year and these would be attracted into the house by the open doors and the super smells of Auntie Beat's cooking. We all took our turns to squash the wasps as they strayed into the windows and a box of matches was kept handy for that purpose. Except one year there genuinely was a veritable plague. Cousin Jane stood on one and stung her foot and, for several days, Auntie Beat said 'George – you really will have to do something about these wasps'. The reply was – as ever – *'Mm-hmm'*. Then, one evening, he was home from harvest work a little earlier than usual. He went to his shed and got some white paint on a small brush. He came into the house to the windows where several wasps were buzzing and picked one up. He took this outside and painted its striped 'sting' with the white paint and walked up the garden before letting it go. It immediately flew off and George hurried to follow it. He knew that a wasp that had been frightened would go to fly back to its nest and he could more easily follow it with its white-painted 'tail'. I was urged to keep away *"Coz they'll get mad at me being around 'em and they'll go crazy and sting anything in soit'*. Having soaked an old hessian sack in paraffin he took it to the nest that

11/8/2012   1:39:29 PM

that question – *'They don't sting me'*. That was it! I guess they did but he was so hard he didn't rate it as pain like the rest of us.

Then there was his accident when he actually saw a doctor AND had a day off work. Up until the 1960s sugar beet was harvested by hand – I can vouch for how cold and tough that task was as it was the first task I was given when, later, I began working on a farm. Beet is lifted from late-September through to after Christmas so the weather is anything that you can imagine – except warm! In those days the roots were lifted and carted to a heap at a field edge (or farmyard if convenient) before being taken to and loaded onto wagons at the local rail station yard if more than six or seven miles from the beet processing factories. The tops or leaves were separated by a beet knife from the roots and left to wilt in the field. Then these tops would be collected by throwing them onto carts with handforks and then be fed to sheep or cattle. In this case a four-wheeled cart had been loaded. Now these carts had large wooden spoked wheels with iron rims about two to three inches wide – so they exerted considerable point pressure upon the ground. The carts themselves would have weighed over two tonnes when empty – look at a local country fair or show next time you see one and check that out. Loaded with sugar beet tops the weight would have been anything up to 10 tonnes – perhaps even more.

George had ridden home from the field in the cart loaded with beet tops. When they reached the farm the tractor driver stopped a bit abruptly on a piece of uneven ground. George couldn't have been concentrating on the interruption to the motion because he fell off the back of the cart – that would have been enough to put most normal souls off work. But that wasn't all. The cart rolled back – and the larger rear iron-clad wheel and then the smaller went to George calling him. George held his stomach and said *'Blast – that bloody thing's hurt me'*. Others came and gathered around and one went and fetched Auntie Beat. After about 10 minutes – during which time George forbade the calling of an ambulance from the Boss's phone at the 'big house' – he asked them to help him get up. A couple supported him and helped him slowly home – some 300 yards. George dismissed them and Auntie cleaned him up and persuaded him to lie on the bed – he managed to get upstairs and that's when the boss arrived to see him. He stood up to George a bit more than most did and insisted that he called the doctor. George spent a bad night in a lot of pain. The doctor arrived after surgery the next morning and examined George who professed he was feeling a lot better than earlier. The doctor was amazed that George wasn't dead and – equally – that he had passed no blood and could not see where any bones had been broken. Even so he could not conceive that anyone could be crushed under the wheels of a loaded cart and not have suffered major abdominal injury. He said that he would get an ambulance to get George to hospital. *'Waste 'a toim'* said George – *'Tell yer what – if oim no better amorrow oill let yer know.'* The doctor felt uncomfortable with this but agreed only by stating that he would call back later that afternoon.

He did call back – and found George on a ladder up the tree in the garden picking the Bramley cooking apples. To the query 'What the devil did he think he was playing at' he got the reply *'Well – oi didn't want the frost to spoil these and oi got so blinking bored just lyin' around'.*

George went back to work as normal the next day.

He did his share of the household tasks and duties though. Even though farm workers always start work earlier than most

I had expended large chunks of my youthful energy running around I rarely awoke before he had left for work – I usually 'joined in the day' when he called in for a quick *'boit o' breakfast'* about half past eight in the mornings. On those occasions when I did wake in time to hear George making his way downstairs first thing I can always remember him issuing a gentle fart as his feet met each step of the stairs. In later years, when teasing him about this, he simply responded *'Yee-a – and oi loiked a good few sneezes as soon as oi got downstairs too – still do'* – and he did!

Another thing at which George excelled was shooting. He had *'Had a gun in moi hand ever since oi can remember'*. When I was about 10 he was home from harvest relatively early one evening and Auntie Beat said that we needed some meat for dinner the next day. He went and picked up his shotgun *'D'you wanna come?'* he asked me – I recall the flush of excitement and pride that this chap had asked me to go with him. It was a lovely sunny, harvest time evening with the sun still emitting its summertime warmth. The cottage that they lived in was towards the lower corner of a largish – 20 acres or so – field. We walked up the sloping field with a thick hedge – which bordered a green lane – on our left to the top boundary of the field where a spindly hedge of mainly elder bushes and a few elm trees formed a thin barrier on a bank. The soil was gravely and there were literally hundreds of rabbit holes in that banked area.

'When we get to the hedge stay behind me in case oi soit a rabbit or somethin'' he warned and as soon as we did he fired and swore as some soil beside the rabbit spurted up. He didn't miss the next one though – and we had our dinner. Holding his boss's permission to shoot on the farm was a literal life saver for the family during the war and after when rationing was so severe and

book to take with me for Auntie Beat.

I remember telling George Horne on the farm that I had been out with Uncle the previous night and that he had sworn when he missed the first rabbit. Mr Horne was really surprised that George had missed and it was then that he told me that he had been the ace shot in the Home Guard in the war (WWII) and had won a couple of competitions for marksmanship. George said as little to me then as he did to everyone else. However, I sidled up to him the next evening as he was getting vegetables from the garden and said 'I didn't know you were such a marvellous shot – Mr Horne told me that you won prizes'. He replied *'That ain't nuth'n'*. I persisted 'Did you shoot anyone in the War then, Uncle?' A pause. *'Can't remember all them years ago'*. Clearly he wasn't in talking mood.

Was he ever in those days?

George smoked all his life – he later admitted it was from the age of about 12 – *'Still most everyone did'* he explained. He always 'rolled his own'. In my lifetime it was always with Empire St Julian tobacco (I still keep nails and screws in tins I collected off him). The thing was he rolled them around his lips and they always showed a brown stain on them. In later years his daughters used to chide him about how disgusting they looked. Inevitably to such complaints they received his classic response – *'Mm-hmm'*. In later years – when he was long retired – he would sit in a comfortable chair and link his fingers across his stomach and, perhaps, doze a little with his fag in his lips. This meant ash would drop onto his shirts and most had very tiny burn marks in them as a result. Another cause for admonishment from Jane and Gill, who washed his clothes after Auntie died, and which may have elicited a bit of an embarrassed chuckle before the inevitable *'Mm-hmm'*. He

27

– and those that he did have were not very good. He eventually had them all out and was given some false teeth. George hated these – and wore them only for a few hours at Gilly's wedding that I can recall – even then he removed them when the food was presented. *'Don't need 'em'* he responded when his daughters told him off – and he didn't. He could chew any type of food as well as people with a full set of perfect teeth. When they attempted shaming him about his appearance with no teeth he would answer by laughing back at his daughters *'Who d'you imagine is goin' to look at me?'* The reply 'Well us for a start…' clearly never impressed him sufficiently to take any notice of their complaints.

As well as being impressed by his capabilities and toughness – which certainly generated something close to awe when I used to go and stay with them – the overriding memory that I can now establish when I think back to my school years was that 'George didn't talk much' – that would gradually alter in years to come.

His daughters filled me in on his family – something, again, he assumed would not be much interest to anyone so was reluctant to talk about. His father was born in the neighbouring village to the south of theirs in 1872 and his mother (Alice) just to the north two years later. His father, Herbert, was a farm worker and George was the third born of eight children. Frances (Fran) arrived in 1895 and she was followed by Arthur in 1897 and George himself two years later on 27th April 1899. Two sisters and three brothers followed and the youngest, Sid, was to die in a motor cycle accident. His youngest sister, Elsie, was to marry my Uncle Joe – brother to my Mum and Auntie Beat. So there were to be two marital links between the Ellis and Wilkin households.

Their home village sits on the main road between Cambridge and Colchester and is a busy route today. Photographs taken early

Made Em Cry.indd   28

11/8/2012   1:39:29

they were.

Chapter Four

◇◇◇

George and Beat married on 27th December 1930. They were then 31 and 27 respectively. Auntie Beat was a nanny meaning that she looked after the children of well-to-do families. She eventually returned to the village as nanny to the family who gave their name to Rose's lime juice and there she met – or possibly re-met – George.

I think of George's wife as a somewhat stern lady. From my childhood period I don't remember her as a 'smiley' sort of person but she was so kind and caring.

She not only welcomed me every summer – and several Easter holidays too – but also looked after one of my Fulham cousins one holiday. This cousin was not really related to Beat either – being daughter of one of my Dad's sisters. Yet Beat treated her as one of the family for a couple of months.

She was such a capable country lady – as most had to be when everything was in such short supply. She was always repairing or making clothes – quite often 'altering' something for me to wear – or knitting. Certainly never idle even though she was not the fittest of women being afflicted with the family 'curse' of asthma which stopped her 'getting her breath' at times.

She was an ace at preserving and preparing food – just thinking about it allows me to recall the smell of something delicious being prepared – I have a waft of plum tart cooking in my nostrils right now!

Although she came over a stern person she was clearly a most kind and generous individual. She and George had two daughters who were very 'can do' and equally generous to their respective families. Both were very capable at sports and Gilly went on to play netball at national level – and umpire at the same high standard when she finally admitted she should stop actually playing.

Being older than me my two cousins tolerated me more than I deserved. I was used to being doted upon by my sister as an 'only child' and had those aggravating mannerisms that, having no competition for people's attention and affection, can bring. While they were very tolerant of me when it came to sports they 'played to win' and I had to get used to being outrun and outplayed by girls. Very character building stuff.

All this Auntie Beat watched over everything with – what I always thought was – a sternish tolerance – George seemed hardly to notice. Amazing when I got older and took my wife to meet Auntie how different she was. Always smiling – just as kind – just how did I get it all so wrong about her character when I was younger?

31

was too young really when cancer claimed her. She had spent some last miserable last days suffering from that curse.

My tolerant wife has had to listen to all my stories of my happy summers in Essex ever since I first knew her. She realised how much Beat and George meant to me and they certainly welcomed her when I took her to meet them.

Somehow it just sort of 'happened' that after Auntie Beat died we should return the compliment to George for all the time over the years that I had spent with them. George, then, would come and stay with us for a few weeks 'in summer'.

This arrangement was eased by the fact that my wife got on so well with George's daughters and their husbands. So, over several years – while we changed homes a number of times – George would come for a few weeks – then a month or so – every year. It gave us a bonus that one of his daughters – almost always Jane and her husband – would bring him up and have a weekend with us and then we would meet up a few weeks later somewhere – have a day together and they would return him home.

It was in this period of our lives that George began to talk and when the experiences recounted here became 'live'.

He was now retired, of course, and his two daughters called in at least once each week each to 'sort him out'. His days then revolved around cycling to his local – The Alma – most lunchtimes for a pint or three and the whisky 'chasers' and a few games of dominoes and a spell of playing the fruit machine inside the door of the bar – something he practised in whatever pub I took him to that had such a machine. He did admit –without prompting – that he hit the jackpot on the fruit machine one day which caused him to celebrate a bit. The extra whisky consumed when Jane or Gill were not calling – he would prepare one of the meals that they had previously taken for him.

He had a minor stroke one year but was soon home again and, as far as his visits to us were concerned, these were unaffected by it as, by summertime, he was fine. And still drinking – and smoking. His daughters were getting more concerned about him now and he had 'slowed down' a bit we noticed.

He became an expert wine maker. His speciality became runner bean wine which he made in massive quantities – at its peak he filled over a hundred empty whisky bottles with the stuff one season. He had emptied the whisky bottles, of course.

To start the wine making process he would grow a couple of rows of runner beans in his now reduced vegetable garden. These he would allow to grow well past their culinary state then pick them and slice the sides of the enlarged beans with a knife before letting them ferment – using an old bath for this process. He spent a lot longer making the stuff than he did drinking it.

When he used to come to stay with us he always had a box containing several bottles of his home-made wine. This he used to consume as a 50-50 mix with whisky – a decent slug too as a bottle of whisky would only last him five or six days. A little while before lunch every day he would get up and fix himself a drink – occasionally two. This he might repeat in the evenings unless sharing a beer with me – when he would just have the whisky 'straight' with his pint. Enjoying his drink never made any difference to his demeanour. He was now 'everyone's favourite uncle'. A kindly, amused, interested and interesting old chap.

He would chat to neighbours if he saw them. Often he would have a stroll around the garden or up the road – wherever we were living – we had four homes in a relatively short span of them than I did.

He simply loved my wife and kept telling me *'What a lovely gal she is'*. That affection was returned.

Similarly he was great with our – then – young sons, joining in with whatever they were doing and they simply accepted that he was there and treated him as a member of our family when he was around. So he got involved in games and would play with them as required. He talked much more than when he worked and during those long summers of my youth.

He seemed to enjoy a game of cards or dominoes with me in the evenings. It seemed that these sessions jogged his memory and brought things back to him. I liked nothing better than – having let the cards rest – he would light one of his fags, lean back in the chair and begin *'Well – no oi-er'* or, of course, 'Well – yes – oi-er'…

Some of what came next you can now read.

CHAPTER FIVE

◇◇◇

We were watching the television news one evening and there was an item about the late Queen Mother celebrating her birthday. We commented to George how well she looked and how fit she appeared whereupon he observed *'Well – she's only a slip of a gal'*. She would have been 80-something that year.

When we asked George after the news what he meant he said *'Well! – she was born in this century oi wasn't'* – this was in the 1980s. When we quizzed him closer he told us that he was born in 1899 whereas the Queen Mother was born in 1900! He considered himself her senior and suggested that he should *'Be on the telly not that young gal'* – and laughed.

George was born in a village in north Essex – the environs of which he rarely left until he 'joined up' in 1917. He was one of a large family typical of the times and, although they never had

10 or 11. Pigeon, hares and, if he could get away with it, pheasants and partridges were regularly on the table for the family. He loved the chance to shoot wild duck too and although demanding much patience that was not a problem for George.

As a boy growing up he confessed to me that he would have been *'Difficult – allus up to somethin'.* Often this was due to him wanting to contribute to the family's plate, sometimes it was just to aggravate somebody or to show daring.

He was not so easy to draw out on his boyhood experiences but admitted to letting 'one old woman's' washing drop to the ground after she moaned to the village 'bobby' about him doing something to annoy her. *'She knew it would've been me but didn't catch me pulling the prop away – but oi did it'*, he confessed, amused still.

Scrumping fruit and vegetables and 'borrowing' people's bikes to slip to an adjacent village – *'Ter see the gals, o' course'* – were regular occurrences. He reckoned that if we looked closely enough we would see his initials carved by penknife at the top of every telegraph pole between his village and the next – he insisted that was so at one stage earlier in the century *'Me'n my old mate did that one spring 'n'summer oi 'member'.*

These simple bits of information leaked out at different times. They don't appear to suggest anything too sinister until, perhaps, he left school which I recount later, but they help to provide the evidence that here was someone who had little fear, did not bother too much about authority but was keen to support the family unit. I guess, too, that these were early indicators that he had a cussed streak in him.

In fact there were reports in the local weekly newspaper of August 1916 of 'young boys' amusing themselves around the village of Ridgewell – where he lived – and causing something of a nuisance.

magistrate the Special Constable also added that he was 'leaving shortly' so the magistrate commented that he hoped that these young people would learn to behave more responsibly and asked 'What will they want next – a merry-go-round – perhaps they will learn to play pitch and toss and cards'. George may not have been part of this group annoying others but it does, somehow, fit with his description of himself when young – *'always up ter somethin'* as he described himself.

George 'joined up' in 1917 but was, initially, placed on reserve awaiting call-up. He eventually was summoned to report to Warley (a depot of the Essex Regiment) in Essex on 13th June 1917. *'Oi quite fancied the Army Service Corps – transport y'know cause oi was used t'horses.'* That wasn't to happen though.

One evening he recounted to me some extraordinary experiences that he had between leaving school, in 1913, and when he joined up. He worked for the Reeve family at Bowes Farm in the village. This was then farmed by Fred and his two sons – the elder, Joe, took over the farm when his father died in July 1914. The farm was 155 acres – no bigger than many modern fields – had a team of horses and a dairy herd from which milk was delivered around the village by 'a boy' with a pony and trap.

Well- yes oi-er – y'see there was the farm workers' stroik at the toim. Oi worked up at Bowles Farm up Ashen Road. We wouldn't go in ter work – but the cowman and the waggoner did – we thought it was all roit fer the cowman to be in there but reckoned the waggoner should come out and leave Fred n' Joe ter look after the hosses.

Corse there was a lot of bad feelin' and after a few days some o' the men were weakening ready ter go back ter work. It was all roit for me, yer see, young, single and no family to feed. Oi was fer stayin' out forever if necessary – at least 'til we got better wages.

was scared stiff o' bein' kicked out of his little old cottage. Well –
some of us young 'uns got one of the wagon ropes off the farm and
we took this poor old boy and trussed him up with this rope. We
then slung him over the railway bridge up Ashen Road and toid it
safe. Every time one o' them old steam trains came through to or
from Birdbrook he had to lift his legs up and got covered in soot and
sparks. We dragged him back 'ventually – poor old tool that he was.
D'yer know though – he still wouldn't stroik – scared stiff o' the boss
he was.

Oi thought later that he must have had a bit o' somethin' about
him though to still go in to work after all that we did to him.

◇◇

That man – the waggoner – was probably Fred Playle because
accounts in the local newspaper for the time show that, in 1916,
Joe Reeve was successful in gaining exemption from being
called up into the forces stating that he was vital to his farming
operation – more of which later.

I had never been aware of a farm workers' strike and had
great difficulty in finding any reference to it. I was aware that
there was a major agrarian revolt in the 1830s and again (with
Joseph Arch urging agricultural workers to become Unionised
in support of better pay and conditions and then the Tolpuddle
Martyrs) in the 1870s but had great difficulty in corroborating
George's reminiscences of 1914 – until I studied the copies of the
local newspaper (*The Halstead Gazette*) for that year. George had
told me that he was on strike and, of course, I could not refer to
him for more information. Fortunately it is all clearly detailed in
the local newspapers for the time.

38

Union (which went through many metmorphosese, eventually became the National Union of Agricultural Workers by the time that I joined in 1957 and is now part of the TGWU). The main causes were disputes about pay – which was then subject to local negotiation in an area or even a village. Pay for a general worker would then vary between 13s (65p) and 15s (75p) for a 54-hour week within a quite small locality. Communications were very limited but word would spread about those who were earning more just a short distance away. Those working on farms in Helions Bumpstead were clearly pretty fed up with their conditions and so they went on strike whereupon their employers locked 23 of them out in March 1914. This caused a furore and much anger and the upshot of this was that many other farm workers in neighbouring villages joined the Union and they too came out on strike. The other villages where the strike was very strongly supported were Birdbrook, Sturmer and Ridgewell – where George and his family lived and were employed.

In the village of Helions Bumpstead – where all this started – other farmers in the locality rode to the farms affected by the walk out and helped them get their hay made and stacked – the local paper refers to scuffles and whippings when strikers tried to prevent that.

Events became very heated and those on strike would cycle to each other's villages to give support and persuade those not yet in the Union to join and come out with them – there is a report that the strikers – which included 15-year-old George – persuaded the boy who delivered the milk for Reeve's to come out and that Reeve's employees were instrumental in getting others in the village to strike – the 'cussedness' of George was being developed! Reeve's employees – including George Ellis – were the strike ringleaders had to be called in to escort those few who refused to strike to work in the village – one, possibly, was the waggoner at Reeve's farm who George had helped to truss up.

Two of the more serious events that occurred were reported in the local press. Two men were discharged for lack of evidence when accused of holding and beating their employer but a further two were committed for trial on a charge of attempted murder – with a revolver – of a farmer. Those two were imprisoned as were two more for assaulting a policeman.

Clearly – there was a lot of ill feeling in the north west Essex area.

The Union demands were for standardised pay of 15s (75p) with working hours regulated to 6am–5pm in summer (with 2 hours for meals) and 7am–5pm in winter with 1½ hours for meals with Saturday afternoons and Bank Holidays off (then just two days/year). They also were demanding 6d per hour (2½p) overtime, three months' tenancy for tied cottages, recognition of the Union and reinstatement of those out on strike. Their strategy was to gather momentum for the strike, to disrupt haymaking (June/July) and harvest (July–September) the busiest times of the year when labour requirements would be at their peak.

It is interesting to note that strikers received 5s a week (25p) from the Union and a similar amount from the Dockworkers Union throughout the months that they were not working – from June 1914 in the case of the Ridgewell workers – and those in that village and neighbouring Birdbrook were reported as being 'solid' in the newspapers of the time.

The way that George recounted his experience of this to me suggests that – although only a boy himself – he was in his element in all of this. It is probably this 'awkwardness' as he

Made Em Cry.indd   40

11/8/2012   1:39:30

conditions in Belgium and France just a few years later.

Sometime later – maybe a few days or weeks even – he joined things up for me by going on:

Oi could tell they were goin' t' give in and go back to work. Oi was getting a bit bolshie by then and didn't give a damn. Yer see – by the beginning o' August it was clear that War was gonner start. Some o' the blokes were keen to go and join up and some o' the steadier ones amongst 'em thought it wasn't roit to leave the harvest to spoil when we were gonner need the food to foit old Jerry.

Anyway – when they were beginning to talk about goin' back to work and one evening oi'd been ter this 'ere meeting at Bumpstead. Ter tell the trooth oi'd hung about a bit after to say a few words to a gal oi loiked the look of. That's how it came that oi was boiking home on me own that toim.

Oi stopped by some stacks at the soid o' the road fer a fag and a bit of a think – it was getting ter be about dark. Oi was feeling a bit mad that the stroik was goin' ter end – oi could see it would now the damned war was comin'. Oi set fire to this stacky'd y'know. Never meant to burn all of it down but the wind got up a bit and that was what happened.

Corse – no one knew oi'd done it but oi'd been a bit of a ringleader with the strike even though oi was only a lad at the toim. So oi 'spose oi would have been a bit of a suspect yer moit say.

◇◇◇

The Halstead Gazette reports that, on Friday 1st August 1914 five stacks of hay and clover on the road between Steeple Bumpstead and Birdbrook were burnt down. They were on the land owned by the man who was also the local postmaster and belonged to livestock). It noted too that the stacks were insured.

The paper goes on to report that police were investigating the incident but that no one had been arrested. We know that no one was ever arrested – because George only ever told me (and *'p'raps one or two old mates in the army'* he was later to tell me) that he had done this. There is need to be clear about this – it was a most serious offence to undertake arson. The Law then prevailing – The Malicious Damages Act of 1861 had been placed on the statute book as a result of such actions against property by those who were either disaffected or plain criminal. I feel sure that George was in the former category but there should be no misunderstanding – if anyone had known that he was responsible for the loss of these stacks he would have been gaoled for a considerable period. It is equally clear that it frightened him – that is why he confided to hardly anyone for another 70 years! He never got involved in anything else remotely serious again as far as I know – unless, of course, his wartime escapades are included.

It is interesting that this localised rural 'revolt' occurred though and how little seems to be formally recorded about it. Certainly food prices had risen leading up to the War due to shortages and farmers were having a much better time of things financially as a result. George clearly had some problems with his employer who he saw as 'tight' or stingy. This was in the period leading up to the massive uprising in Russia where the Bolsheviks took over and the monarchy disappeared. Times were changing and the growth of the middle classes – or perhaps the beginning of the middle class – was apparent really for the first time. George's experiences, I now realise, were symptomatic of those changes which were occurring internationally.

by during that month. The riots in those three villages – which began on 1st December 1830 – featured demands for food and beer and was quelled by a small raise in weekly wage rates which dispersed the gathered groups by 3rd December. These were more than localised events though being part of the so-called 'Swing' agrarian revolt which began in Kent and affected much of England and Wales. In many areas any machinery was broken by mobs of dissenters but this was mainly aimed at thrashing machines which were seen as the cause by many workers of the loss of their traditional winter-time income – thrashing had previously been a wintertime hand work task. However incendiarism formed a large feature of that revolt and this act of defiance/rebellion remained a fairly common means for Essex rural dwellers to display their anger and frustrations for many years after. The so-called 'Swing' movement was rather different – letters warning of proposed action against farmers and landowners were often sent in advance by a letter from the ubiquitous 'Captain Swing' – some of these were very intimidatory in nature and sometimes threatened bodily harm on the recipient and even his family and workers. This whole movement and revolt morphed into the well-documented Tolpuddle Martyrs crusade and the formation of formal trade unionism in the 1860s and 70s.

Now there could have been no one still living who took part in the 1830 revolt in 1914. However, there could well have been some 'history' – which might have become ingrained into local folk lore – that would help to explain why this quiet north west 'corner' of Essex – in particular George's home village of Ridgewell – featured so prominently in 1914. It might also explain where any thoughts of firing stackyards or property might have originated.

deep trouble. The amazing thing to me was that he told me that I was the only person – other than, possibly, one or two mates in the army – that he had ever confessed that to. If anyone in the locality remembered the stacks burning down he was absolutely sure that they wouldn't know that he had started it.

His cussedness would also help to explain, to some extent, how he came to survive the War and still be alive to recount some of his experiences all those years later. One thing that has often made me ponder on this bolshie streak in his character though is that he wasn't necessarily anti-authority. For example I can never recall him complaining or really criticising officers from his time in the army. There has been much written about the apparent follies of the 'top brass' but their actions were not something that appeared to bother George at all. I find that rather odd given how willing he was to admit to his cussedness and obstinacy. He never really complained about police or the lawmakers so it is difficult to think he was against rules and regulations in general.

George never said if he knew anything of the French Army Mutiny in 1917 when the front line troops informed the French High Command that they would defend their lines against any German attack but would not take part in any aggressive action. It seems that the Germans knew nothing of this rebellion against – what were seen by the French troops – as orders to carry out, what they saw as, ill-directed attacks which prevailed between May and September of 1917 and only changed when Marshal Foch took overall command and the German assaults in 1918 had been repelled. This was yet another example of the changes in attitude towards 'the upper/ruling class' that were increasingly prevalent at this time and were fuelled by front line experiences.

year. Reports to that effect were made in March of 1915 but this obviously did not match the overwhelming body of opinion because no such organised disputes appeared to have taken place. The Great War – and an increase in wages to 17s (70 pence) per week in the Colne Valley area of Essex from that year – seems to have weakened resolve and interest in industrial action – as it is termed nowadays. Despite the unrest in Russia and elsewhere George was never again involved in such a dispute.

CHAPTER SIX

◇◇

The staggering losses that occurred in France and Belgium and the lack of any signs that the war might end in any reasonable time led to the passing of The Military Service Bill in late 1915 which effectively meant that any able-bodied man over 18 years of age was eligible for military service. This stated that farmers themselves would be exempted from military service together with key workers as long as they were married and such exemption was approved by local Tribunals set up to hear such cases.

At that time the overwhelming majority of the population outside of the major cities worked in agriculture. In World War Two, some 25 years later, many farm workers were exempted from military service given the critical shortage of food stocks caused by the War effort and the German U-Boat blockade. These exemptions did not automatically apply in World War One. Partly because such a large

Government Secretary of State for War, Lord Derby, issued a call for women to help fill some of the roles that many typically undertook. This helped to fuel the change of the role of women in society and increased the demands for electoral emancipation. This is another indicator of the seismic changes in society that the war helped to bring about. There were even moves to assess men with declared disability to see if they could undertake some of the work on farms and other industries vacated by those being called into the services.

As indicated above, employers applying to get their workers exempted had to appear before a tribunal. If successful these were usually only granted for a specific period – generally three or six months – and a renewal of the exemption would then have to be sought.

It is clear, from press reports, that it was not straightforward to gain a successful judgment. In fact reports of the proceedings suggest that the attitudes of the chairmen of such tribunals meant that the odds against success were high. A typical exchange from one Essex appeal provides indication of the mindset of those sitting in judgment:

Farmer: I could employ another six men if they were available.

Chairman: The Army could employ a million more – appeal dismissed.

◇◇

This whole subject of war service exercised the mind of every fit man. There were attempts made to get a more consistent approach to the decision making process on exemptions – particularly in agriculture. Indeed one Essex farmer had taken the trouble hearing such appeals in Essex were being very harsh on the agricultural industry compared to other counties. He quoted that in Sussex the guideline of four workers/100 acres was considered a reasonable ratio whereas in Essex a rough figure of two men/100 acres appears to have been adopted. Skilful and diligent the claimant may have been in constructing his case but his appeal was still rejected by the chairman!

Although Ridgewell may have been a 'hotbed' of dissent during the farm workers' strike in 1914 its inhabitants were certainly not reluctant to enter war service. *The Halstead Gazette* published a 'league table' by parish of the numbers of men who volunteered prior to the passing of the Military Service Act. Ridgewell was positioned fifth in a list of 50 parishes having 12 per cent of the then recorded population of 455 adults who had volunteered to serve before the generalised mobilisation became Act of Parliament.

The paper also recorded names of those who had died in the fighting – one poignant entry on that list was Arthur Ellis of the 5th Essex Territorials – George's eldest brother.

He spoke several times of the prevailing attitude in those times – of how it was a *'bit of a laugh – an adventure'* in 1914 and 1915 until the death toll began to become clear. The losses could not be escaped – every single week from August 1914 onwards obituaries to those who had died appeared in the local paper – of which George would most certainly have been aware. A fairly jingoistic stance was taken by the local press initially although this clearly softened after about mid-1916 when the horrors of the events in the near-Continent became too obvious and uncomfortable.

This encouraging attitude was exemplified by the regular publication of poems and verses supposedly written 'at the front' by some of our 'brave men and boys'. These were intended to quoted as an example of the sort of exhortation that appeared during the first two years of the war in the papers:

I wish to heaven that you could see two men in my platoon
I watched them from my dug-out all one afternoon
I thought of all the men at home whose ages came between
This fine old man of fifty-four – this child of seventeen

The rain was coming down in sheets: they didn't seem to mind
They walked about & searched for any wood that they could find
They laughed & joked & whistled tunes & each one took a turn
At lighting up a little fire that quite refused to burn

Their patience & their cheerfulness as they stood there in
the mud
Well – somehow seems to drive one mad & make them thirst
for blood
Of slackers now in England who are the first to shirk
While 'fifty-four' and 'seventeen' come out to do their work

Yet George said he never for one moment considered not going into the army when called to do so. He was enlisted under the Act in 1916 and became part of the army reserve at that point. He would have sworn his allegiance and been attested and medically examined. He received his mobilisation orders and reported to Great Warley in Essex (near Brentwood – in fact it is alongside the modern time M25 London Orbital Road) on 13th June 1917 probably on the strength, initially, of the Essex Regiment whose base was at that site. He was then accepted for military service for the duration of the war and was sent to Rugeley to undergo his training.

49

would face.

So our lively, active, sometimes 'cussed' farm labourer became a soldier.

CHAPTER SEVEN

◇◇

Soon after our small sons had broken up for the summer holidays one year George arrived with us in our, then, Warwickshire home. We showed him their school reports and he said how impressed he was with their teachers' comments.

Course oi wasn't up ter much at school – didn't foind things so difficult – just didn't see the point of a lot of the stuff they troid ter teach us. Oi knew oi'd just be working on the land all me loif so was much more interested in learning ter do things- somethin' useful – instead o' reading about 'em. Soon as it came to doin' something oid step forrrard and do it – that were me as a youngster.

We talked a bit about his schooldays – *'Allus in the village school – a big gang of us from about foive or six up to 'bout 14'*. He didn't often play truant as *'Everyone would soon've known about it'* but loved any excuse to go and do something on the farm –

51

didn't feel that academic issues were much use to him. Later in life he was a keen reader of a newspaper and kept in good touch with what was going on around him in the world and would join in any conversation on most topics. So he had an ever-active brain capable of – what many in their eighties are not – joining in any sort of discussion.

We talked one evening about what we might do with our two boys the next day and we mentioned taking them back to Cannock Chase in Staffordshire where they loved to run wild in the heavily forested area. George jerked up and said *'Chase? That's where oi trained when oi joined up'*.

Well, of course, that settled it, trying to locate where George was camped in 1917 would add extra excitement to a day on Cannock Chase. Off we went, armed with our picnic the next day and we looked at several areas of this huge sandy-soiled – and largely wooded – area and once came to a large cleared expanse. George thought given the gently sloping west-facing view that *'It moit have been it'*. Naturally in an area where trees are continually felled and replanted it is very difficult to revisit an area just even a few years later and be sure that it is the same spot that you saw last time. Nevertheless we had a good day out and it prompted him to recall some of his memories of the area and his period of army training over the days that followed our day out.

Cannock Chase is a large area owned then by the Earl of Lichfield who then resided at nearby Shugborough Hall. As the need for more men grew three huge training camps were created on the Chase – Penkridge, Brocton and Rugeley. There were some 40,000 men a time in training there from 1916 onwards. George arrived on Cannock Chase on 1st August 1917 to join 1st on 1st December 1917.

Anyhow, George – as well as our boys – enjoyed his trip and, as I suspected it might, it set his memories rolling over the next few days. These are some of the comments that he made and events that he recalled over several days that followed.

Well, no oi-er… we lived in all these wooden huts with a little old coke burner in the middle of it – full o' fumes the hut was but some of the blokes felt the cold – never affected me much o' course.

Some of us were just farm boys that had never been away from our villages afore. Loads of 'em were from towns – Yorkshire and Manchester way an' that. It was them townies that felt the cold a bit and a few were even scared about going out in the dark – which let them in fer a bit of ribbing.

We seemed ter spend most of our days standing around being told or shown things and getting frozen stiff. Some never did pick up the marching – oi didn't moind it – at least it warmed yer up a bit. They poor old boys who couldn't tell left from roit got a real ear bashing from the NCOs though. PT was all roit and musketry – as they called rifle drill – was easy for me – they soon learnt that oi could hit most anything with a gun.

They taught us gas warfare and that began ter show us that this wadn't just a game and that it was damned serious stuff over there in France. Throwin' grenades was good stuff – 'though there was some nasty accidents with these when blokes panicked – a few got killed at practice. Oi got on well with most o' the training – enjoyed scouting but never got much of a chance at signalling 'cos they had me down as a snoiper pretty quick. In the end though they got me marked down as a roifle bomber and that is what oi got some extra training in – though oi learned when oi 'ventually got out there just survivin' was what yer needed to know most about.

53

toim at the front loin and some reckoned that they were going back with us to foit. They seemed keen ter troi to knock us into shape in case we had got to work with 'em when we got over there.

The officers though – well that was odd – took a bit o' getting used to. Most of seemed about the same age as us and just as green. 'Cept they spoke with a posh accent as they were from public schools and university and all that. They certainly seemed ter be a bit more used ter being in a group than we did but didn't know any more about warfare than us. Tell the truth – oi felt more confident of the NCOs than oi did of most of the officers – though oi soon learned when we got out there that they were treated just as rough as we were.

We 'ventually began ter feel a bit more loik soldiers and started ter look for a bit o' fun when off duty. We tended ter group in the old YMCA hut for a start but then gradually some of us branched out a bit. They had marched us through town one day to show the locals how smart we were oi s'pose. Lot o' women loined the streets to wave and some o' they young 'uns were real sporty – several jumped out and gave those of us marching closer to the kerb a quick peck on the cheek – oi quite enjoyed that! Oi s'pose a big group o' strange young blokes would seem excoitin' if you had never been far from home y'self.

A few of us talked about those young gals and thought that we would get down to town one evening to meet up with 'em though we were told that the MPs patrolled round town. 'ventually we did – at least oi did.

I remember it was some time later when George completed his story of his training period – this was, typically, of about 14 weeks' duration. When Lloyd George became Prime Minister in 1917 he promised that he was going to end the war and reduce the losses occurring in France and Belgium. For a while he stopped fresh troops going over to France and this meant George's lot had a the 'A4' men – trained and fit but not yet 'of age' to go to the front line. At that stage – 1st December 1917 – he was transferred to the 4th Reserve Battalion of the Duke of Wellington's (West Riding) Regiment before being moved to the Regiment's 3rd (Reserve) Battalion which was posted to North Shields to man coastal defences of the Tyne estuary and to continue training. (There had also been some Zeppelin raids and the Germans were beginning some strikes with their Horsa bombers along the East Coast of England).

Maybe even not on that particular stay with us but at some point he went on to tell me about a particular lady:

…funny enough she wasn't one o' them that watched us march into the town though there were a good few loinin' the streets when we got there.

She was a widow – husband had been killed down a moin. Oi saw her walking along – she'd been to see her husband's mother – and so oi hung back a bit from me mates to speak to her. It were very dark that evening but she didn't seem scared or anythin'. Oi walked along with her 'til she said that this is where she lived and oi said oi would call boi and see her again – oi was surprised when oi thought about it 'cause she just said 'All roit'. See – oi knew she was older than me – oi was just a slip of a boy then really.

Well – any noit that oi could oi went to see her – tell the truth we were both a bit upset when oi told her we were off sometime in the next few days. Y'know boi – she were moi first proper girl – just been schoolboy stuff 'afore her oi reckon.

Oi never made a lot of it to the others 'cause they moit have given me a bit of leg pull – oi just slipped away quietly loik. Just kept it to meself – but it made all those long hours stood around a bloomin' old gun a lot more bearable!'

ade Em Cry.indd   55

11/8/2012   1:39:31 PM

– awaited them. Being passed fit for overseas duty in March 1918 George landed in Boulogne on 31st March and went to a nearby hutted camp (No.6 Infantry Base Depot). The Germans had made – what history now tells us was their last 'big push' and Lloyd George had agreed to send the recently trained reserves to try to help hold them and prevent them taking Paris and reaching the Channel ports. At the point George landed in France total devastation of the Allies was a very real possibility as a result of the considerable gains that the Germans were making.

Just two days after arrival he was transferred to the 2nd Battalion of the York & Lancaster Regiment and received his fourth army number in little more than a year! This explains – what had always been a mystery to his family – as to how he came to be in a northern Regiment. Due to the enormous losses incurred at the front it was common that almost all new trainees were posted on arrival in France/Belgium according to need – it was nothing unusual for this to happen. Thus, George became Private 46174 – a rifle bomber (the specialism to which he had been trained on Cannock Chase) of the 2nd Battalion of the York & Lancaster Regiment. It was significant that he received no front line training on his arrival (although he did later) in France which gives some idea of the extent of the panic that then applied to the last big German advance that George, and others like him, went more-or-less straight into action in the trenches on arrival from Britain.

CHAPTER EIGHT

I cannot be sure where my admiration for those who serve in our armed forces comes from. Perhaps there have been a number of sublime influences upon me that have helped to fashion my attitude.

Possibly it is the fact that, during my younger childhood, my father would often take me to watch the changing of the guard at Buckingham Palace – I can recall the thrill when, for the first time, I saw the guards in dress uniform after the war as they had always been in khaki up until then. Maybe this helped spark my admiration.

Of course the presence of the military was very much more apparent in the years at the end of World War Two – particularly for those of us living in London where national celebrations tend to be held. There was still a pride – as well as relief – that Germany and Japan had been defeated during my childhood and society

– I have always basked in reflected pride of the fact that he held every rank in the army from Private up to Major.

Maybe it was the Biggles-type stories that I read in my youth that fired my respect for those who serve our nation.

Perhaps, too, it was the embarrassment I felt when National Service conscription into the armed forces ceased just 10 months before I would have been called-up when many of my near-contemporaries at school had had to do their 'two years' of conscription.

Certainly my respect and pride in the armed forces has its origins long before George singled me out as the confidant for his reminiscences. In fact I have often thought that the dismissive way that he always dealt with the horrors of war at first made me somewhat ashamed when – years after his death – claims of post-traumatic stress became quite openly accepted as a consequence of front line duties. At first I suppose that I subconsciously considered those afflicted as some sort of 'weaklings' and not worthy of the uniform they wore. Reading so much of World War One – and other conflicts since, has made me totally sympathetic to people so affected but it wasn't George who made me so.

George had always made it clear to me that he simply accepted the awful brutality that war brings. He accepted too the discomfort that being in the forces – indeed all aspects of life – threw at him. *'No good moaning – just get on with it'* would be his watch-phrase – I heard him use that expression, or something similar, any number of times. Goodness knows when or how he became so mentally, as well as physically, tough. It may have been based on that confessed cussed streak in him tempered with growing up in a large family with limited financial resources and domestic comfort.

been the little matter of a shared 'liking of the ladies' that helped forge their companionship. The fact that a more experienced soldier took George 'under his wing' suggests that he recognised in George someone who just accepted things as they were and uncomplainingly carried on. It has struck me that he must soon have become close to George because he recognised him as a substitute sniper within a few days of George being posted alongside him whereas George was really a rifle bomber so George must have displayed his accuracy with a rifle pretty quickly.

I could never get George to talk about actual life in the trenches too much – he would admit that they were 'terrible places' and that the rats and lice were difficult to describe. He did once admit horror at watching rats feeding off dead soldiers until the bodies could be brought in after dark. Once, when prompted a little he did admit:

… yes – when we did first get near the front line for the first toim it seemed like total madness and chaos – and the noise well, yer couldn't believe. Oi 'member rushing around as we got near the front a bit excited loik – ter get a better look what it was all loik. Yet oi 'member the very next day, during a lull, just getting moi head down and droppin' off to sleep just where we stopped. Oi just seemed ter get used to it straightaway – oi don't know woi. But then – it were all terrible. Allus a stink o' some sort too – gas lingered and allus the stink of the dead – men and animals. Shellholes often full o' stinking yeller, glue – and no end o' blokes doid by drownin' in 'em yer know. No – yer just don't want ter know, oi'll tell yer that much.

I wonder what he would have made of post-traumatic stress syndrome? He never seemed to run down those less strong than he never disparaged those less tenacious or more sentimental than he was. So – quite probably, I think – he would have accepted the fact that some people were more affected by trauma than he was and would have thought no less of them because of that.

I feel that that would probably be the case because – especially when I was younger – whenever I told him how brave I thought he must have been he always brushed such comments aside. He quickly pointed out that there were millions of men just the same as him who 'did their bit', returned home afterwards and led a perfectly normal life. He always said that what he did was nothing more than anyone else and that, as proof, he never got any special medals or anything like that. After all he reckoned he was only there *'as things started ter come ter an end – though it were a bit rough fer a woil when old Jerry were a-pushin'.'* He soon learned to adopt a pragmatic approach to fighting – as he admitted when he never sought to repeat his sniping accuracy that he demonstrated near Zillebeke (see later) he was 'green' then and would rather 'warn old Jerry to behave himself' rather than kill them. He just concentrated on trying to stay alive and stuck as close to his 'old corporal' as he reasonably could.

Well, yes… … oi reckoned that if oi stayed close to old corp' he wouldn't let me down. O' course that led us ter some dirty damned jobs. I hated fetching the wounded in from in front o' the trenches or puttin' up fresh woir but he often seemed to volunteer for that sort o' thing. Bloody Jerries – and sometimes our lot – would send up flares when yer were out there and oi felt sure that everyone in the whole damned world could see me – enough to froiten the loif out o' yer. Oi always felt that oi ought ter go though 'cause oi reckoned that oi would want someone to do the same for me when oi bought my lot.

and NCOs would read at night to go and capture Germans from
their front trenches for interrogation. I told him that I had read about that – *'Mm-hmm'* – was his less than eloquent response. All I got from him was *'Used ter happen a lot the other way round as well, y'know'*.

Clearly – that was an off-limit topic and I never went back to that with him although he did recount one incident which I report later. This also suggests that retribution and vengeance were not motivating factors that helped George to cope with front line duty – and hatred of the enemy certainly wasn't. Supporting those he lived alongside and doing his share of things seem to have been important to him. Of course, it could have been that he never analysed his method of 'coping' – or just never spoke of it.

His acceptance of all that was happening around him, (no matter how awful), his tolerance of other people's weaknesses and limitations all suggest to me that he would not have thought ill of those whose lives have been more adversely affected by their experiences of battle. He also possessed the valuable ability to use something pleasant – or less terrible, at any rate – to help him deal with whatever it was he had to put up with – a useful character trait which many must wish that they possessed.

So I still admire those who serve our country and protect its interests and I pray that those who are mentally as well as physically scarred by their experiences of so doing gain peace and comfort for doing what I would never be brave enough to do.

Somehow George never seemed to need those sentiments – or if he did he was brilliant at covering them up.

George's reluctance to talk about some parts of his experience to me (and any part of it to anyone else) mirrors exactly the attitude of other veterans of World War One. In recent times two wonderful survivors waited until around their respective 100th and why he told me anything still amazes me to this day – but I consider myself infinitely richer for the fact that he eventually did so. The association that this gave me may partly explain my admiration for those who fight for us today as well as those who endured any part of those dreadful years between 1914 and 1918 in Belgium and France.

Made Em Cry.indd   62

11/8/2012   1:39:31

CHAPTER NINE

◇◇◇

Trying to make sense of George's war experiences and visiting the villages and areas mentioned in his surviving Regimental Battle Orders highlighted to me just how ignorant I was about World War One.

Names of places/battles were indelibly imprinted on my mind but I admit to being in a total mental 'fog' how they all fitted together. I realised that, if George's recollections were going to mean anything at all to me – let alone anyone else – that I had better get more of an understanding just where and when the 'first/second/third battles' of various places took place and just where all those places, that a lifetime of general reading had imprinted in my mind, actually are. Where do Ypres, Paschendale, the Messines Ridge, Vimy Ridge, The Somme, St Quentin, Albert and all the rest fit in? In the end I learned that not all featured in

A potted resume may help others to better understand where dates and names fit together but, of course, a student or someone wishing to be better informed needs to read detailed accounts by historians rather than that of a mere nephew of someone who served on the two main British-held fronts towards the end of hostilities! The image on pages 98 to 99 may also assist those who, like me found the chronology and geography of the First War confusing or unclear.

When the German army swept through Belgium on its way to France (between the Dutch and Luxembourg borders) in 1914 they made rapid progress and soon skirted round and crossed the defensive Maginot Line which the French had hoped would prove impregnable. The British army first entered battle near the Belgium town of Mons which is south west of Brussels not so far from the French border. Much of these first contacts were skirmishes often involving cavalry but, within a few days, it was clear that modern artillery and machine guns were going to call for a different approach due to the appalling losses suffered. Eventually, the Allies managed to halt the German advance on a north-south line that stretched from Ypres in the north, through Arras, Amiens to about 50km east of Paris before eventually swinging east to the town of Verdun and hence slightly south again to the Swiss border some 450 miles (720km). The advance was halted by September of 1914 as a result of lines of trenches being dug – in a meandering 'S' shape along the axes mentioned and shown on the map on pages 98 to 99 – and by some exhaustion of men and supplies on the German side.

Basically the British took responsibility for the northern part of the line (being nearer to the Channel ports) and the French further south with the final dividing line being around The Somme

64

Verdun) were never taken or held by the Germans throughout the war although much of the ground between the two was taken and retaken many times during those terrible years.

There were some deadly exchanges of ground and, over the next two years or so, the gains that were made – at huge cost of life – by the Allies by the end of 1916 meant that the front line had moved a little east in the northern sector and rather more further south. But really the two years to 1916 were largely an attritional stalemate with some fearsome local fighting but only modest movement by either side.

Between main campaigns there was a pattern of near-continuous artillery bombardment and fierce local battles to attempt to gain quite minor pieces of ground. But in late 1916 and early 1917 the Allies made their 'big push' predominantly in the central areas where the Allied and French lines met – in Picardy more commonly termed 'The Somme' from the river of that name which traverses that area. Gains were achieved but much of these were due to the Germans deciding to fall back onto some well-prepared defensive positions – which they termed the Hindenburg Line in Picardy, in particular. On that line the advance petered out in early summer of 1917. It is this activity that gained The Somme its terrible reputation for slaughter.

Again, bitter localised fighting occurred but the next main offensive was German in the spring of 1918 when they were able to introduce fresh, trained troops freed by their truce in the east with Russia. The focal point of this offensive was where the British and French command met (between the towns of Arras and Flesquenes in Picardy) and where the French trenches were in poor repair (Second Battle of The Somme). At the time the Germans used new tactics (see Chapter 10) and concentrated on

65

Paris increasingly coming under threat – again the map on pages 98 to 99 helps to visualise these dispositions. Then the Allies managed to hold the advance eventually just east of Amiens. The Germans were exhausted and then, in the Spring of 1918 the Allied forces, soon to be boosted by American troops, began their Spring Offensive (Third Battle of The Somme). While costly in men and equipment this succeeded in a near-continuous, hard-earned rolling-back of the German line so that, in November 1918 they sued for peace and the Armistice was called with the front line running just east of Ghent in the north to just east of Mons (where the British had started fighting in 1914) to just west of Sedan and, again, just east of Verdun in the south.

Concentrating on the front which the British generals controlled, it is difficult, at first, to understand why the traditional Belgian town of Ypres – famous then for the excellence of its cloth – is so deeply etched in the British psyche. As a boy my Dad had often spoken about 'Wipers' or 'Eeps' as many called it so it was always a familiar place name to me and to many others. Following generations still stand beneath its impressive Menin Gate for the last post played at 8pm every evening but why is this at Ypres and nowhere else?

The reason for the familiarity with Ypres may first be discerned by looking at the map on pages 98 to 99. Ypres is found about 40km south east from the port of Dunkirk. It is in a flat quite low-lying area which is extensively drained to permit agriculture to be practised. As the German army advanced in 1914 Belgian drainage engineers opened the sluices on their drains north of Ypres. This flooded the land north of the town to the Channel coast making it impassable – at least to large numbers of troops. The first bit of drier land south of this was, of course, around men died or were mutilated in this immediate area over four years and the town itself was quite destroyed although the main area, with its wonderful Cloth Hall, has since been restored with great care.

The British attempted their big campaign in 1916-1917, but around Ypres gained only a quite modest amount of ground – especially when balanced against the massive loss of life suffered. Between 31st July and 10th November 1917 (sometimes termed 'the 3rd Battle of Ypres') the British and Commonwealth troops made slow and bloody progress to the ridge by Paschendaele. When the Germans advanced again in the Spring of 1918 in just three days they pushed the British back almost to where their 1916–17 campaign had started from and it is at this frantic and confused point that George went into the front line. He and his colleagues were soon pushed back to the line held by their colleagues two years before – a sea of total carnage and mud with virtually no buildings or trees and with men living either totally or partly underground to attempt to escape the worst of the near-continual shelling. If ever the term 'hell on earth' was aptly phrased then this must have been one of its most appropriate applications.

The term 'Flanders Fields' is frequently used to signify this northern part of the front. Although a countryman all his life George did say that he saw very little evidence of fields as *'the shellin' had just churned everythin' inter a stinking gluepot'*. The area just south east of Ypres, where George first saw action, was heavily fought over with, as stressed, only modest gains by either side. The 2nd York & Lancasters were mainly positioned between the ruins of the town and the dreaded Messines Ridge – an area of slightly higher ground south east of Ypres. This topography emphasises

67

11/8/2012 1:39:31 PM

it. The Ypres-Commines Canal runs through the area and it can be assumed that this would have contributed to the morass that existed – see the map of Ypres Salient on page 100. Now – add to that – trenches and continual bombardment by both sides and it truly is a wonder that the land was ever restored to anything like the 'normality' that can be seen today, although, mud is never far away as I discovered when I visited the site nearly a century later.

Having halted the big German advance in the late spring of 1918 the 2nd York & Lancasters were moved to Picardy – generally called The Somme – although travelling north east through the town of St Quentin the ground conditions do change. Seen today the area is very reminiscent of the Wiltshire/Hampshire downs – gently rolling and stony. It is devoid of hedges and has few trees although some copses are beginning to mature now to break up the wide, almost featureless landscape which modern agriculture has done little to improve.

George's Regiment were at first 'in reserve' when they were moved to The Somme (Australian troops made the first breakthrough near St Quentin) but quickly into action when the Allies' big breakthrough of the heavily-defended and reinforced German Hindenburg Line was eventually achieved. After this point, although there were still terrible days when thousands died, the war did move more quickly as the Allies gradually rolled the exhausted Germans back during 1918.

So the 'First Battle of Flanders/The Somme' tends to refer to the big German advance in 1914 following the start of hostilities. The 'Second Battles' tend to refer to the Allied offensives in 1916–17 and the 'Third Battles' relate to the German advance in the spring of 1918 and their subsequent collapse as that year wore on. These generalisations may not be universally agreed by scholars of the on pages 98, 99 and 100 help to illustrate the localised extent of these campaigns.

CHAPTER TEN

◇◇◇

The fact that so many men were killed is almost beyond credibility. One in eight British/Commonwealth troops who entered the line died. The horror of it all has to be stressed – it cannot – and I suppose should not – be avoided. Many of these deaths are simply not recorded. So many died as a result of shelling that meant that there were, frankly, no body remains to mark the death. Many of the bodies that were found could not be identified because of obscene mutilations.

World War One is estimated to have cost Britain over £9 billion and created over 350,000 orphans and 200,000 widows – in fact the 1921 census showed that there were towards two million more women in the country than men as a result of the carnage – most of which occurred on what is generally known were ill-informed, too remote from the men and the conditions under which they were fighting and poorly trained for the type of warfare that developed. All that may or may not be true and controversy will probably never completely disappear. What history tells us is that almost all wars that the British army was involved with after the Napoleonic Wars ended in 1815 were pretty miserable debacles at least initially until leaders came in tune with the prevailing circumstances. Those leading our armies in any number of conflicts almost always suffered quite awful, and often humiliating defeats, before learning the lessons and bringing our, then, greater industrial might to bear. Sudan, Zulu and Boer Wars and Indian fighting all showed that our leaders were slow to come to terms with the more mechanised ways of waging war. So it would not be totally surprising that our generals were not ready for what was needed in Belgium and France from 1914.

There had always been a tendency for birthright to decide who led the armed forces. There was more of a meritocracy in the navy where career advancement was more likely to be linked to ability but, in truth, this did not fully apply until well into World War Two in the army. This does not mean that there were no capable officers in 1914–17 just that there were likely to have been a higher ratio of 'duffers'.

George never expressed criticism of the hierarchy of the army that I can recall – again, he probably found it simpler to just accept the situation he found himself in and 'got on with it'.

(Sir – later Earl) Douglas Haig took over from Sir John French (who had been a soldier for 45 years so must have been influenced more by mounted cavalry supporting infantry than massive artillery bombardment and machine guns) in December one man's view is worth, that he was saddled with an inflexible French master-plan for the pursuance of the war, was not always well served by local commanders and was too concerned with being aggressive. The truth is that, immediately after the War, he was hailed as a hero, knighted, helped to establish the British Legion, (for which many ex-service personnel and the families have much to be thankful for to this day), and that the great public outpouring of grief at his public funeral in January 1928 was absolutely massive. The passage of time has diminished his reputation but there are, perhaps thankfully, some historians who are prepared to argue on his behalf.

Certainly anyone with a military background would have struggled to do much better as C-in-C of the Allied forces in World War One. Those who have chosen to criticise Haig tend to be those who seek to defend their own reputations and to cover up their own errors and I think there is a strong case for saying that those who have claimed that they would have done better than Haig were quietly relieved not to have been chosen to try to do so. Indeed, when Lloyd George sent Smuts and Hankey to find someone more capable than Haig to take over from him they failed to find anyone to do so in the whole of the Army!

Certainly Haig made errors – he was always too confident that German morale was about to collapse and that 'one more push' would yield the big breakthrough. His obstinacy in insisting that Paschendale be taken in Flanders became a quite monstrous millstone to weigh down his image as it led to huge losses for little strategic gain. However, anyone trying to weld together the scant remains of the professional army – largely lost in 1914 – with Kitchener's new army of volunteers and then the green conscript army, of which George was part, would have had no easy task.

Made Em Cry.indd   72

11/8/2012   1:39:31

line against his better judgment as he knew he was short of sufficient artillery or men to make a really decisive impact.

In addition Haig had to contend with political confusion at home which often suffered paralysing bureaucratic confusion – perhaps inevitable in a Coalition Government such as that which Lloyd George led. His position in relation to the French – who always had overall tactical control – meant that Haig often had to commit Allied troops when he knew they were not in a sufficiently strong position to carry out what the French asked of them or him.

There are, however, too many examples of poor coordination and inappropriate planning for comfort. I expect that this is the case in any military conflict but a study of the war – and others before and since – suggest that there was no British strategist worthy of note (possibly excluding Kitchener) from 1815 until 1942. If there were then I have simply read the wrong books – or misinterpreted them!

When the British first used tanks – at Cambrai – in November 1917 they were poorly deployed and insufficient advantage was gained from their deployment. When tunnellers created passageways below German defensive positions, and filled these with explosives, (ammonal – similar to TNT was used), the huge detonations were often not well followedup and any potential advantage was dissipated. British tactics became very sterile – typically, a prolonged artillery bombardment, creeping towards the enemy followed by infantry 'going over the top' (crawling out of their trenches and advancing over badly torn ground towards the enemies' positions). There are examples – later in the war – of good local advances achieved with better coordination between tanks and infantry, air support and smoke screens followed up

73

British – in part due to their leaders being less influenced by rigid, outdated tactics than their British counterparts.

The Germans were much more determined to construct strong defensive positions which, too frequently, remained intact after a bombardment. This meant that they could return from deeply dug underground shelters into the prepared machine-gun positions to harass the infantry now heading towards them through the mass of barbed-wire entanglements, shell holes and, often, mud. If they did lose control of a trench they typically appear to have mounted well-directed counter-attacks more quickly and effectively than the Allies did after a German advance until towards the end of fighting.

Particularly after 1918 the German attacks were much more appropriately planned and applied. They would use lightly armed stormtroopers using flame throwers, light mortars, light machine guns and rifle grenades to create a breach that could be held and then use this as a bridgehead in the line to isolate defensive positions through which they quickly poured more troops causing the Allies to quickly fall back or run the risk of being attacked from behind by encircling forces. Additionally, as mentioned, the British trenches and defensive positions, especially, were much less well prepared because Field Marshal Haig was always offensively minded and considered that he was always on the brink of a big breakthrough which meant that it was not appropriate to build such elaborate defences. Having said that there were some extensively prepared underground bunkers – like small villages in some cases – prepared by the Royal Engineers particularly in the area around Ypres – but here the War was much more stationary. However, generally, the Germans prepared their positions more thoroughly.

74

11/8/2012 1:39:32

dug them. In Flanders, as mentioned, the soil was mainly of heavy clay so this prevented the surface water permeating too deeply into the underground positions. Two timber-lined shafts would be dug for each bunker and the tunnels underneath would have steel girders to support the roof and the walls would be lined with corrugated steel sheeting or timber. Gas curtains would drape the entrances at top and bottom of the stairwells/entrances. Trench pumps would then be used to remove any water that did seep through up to the surface. These bunkers would be 13-14m deep and about 50 people would be housed there as a control HQ or mess with kitchens and communications hubs being contained in these below-ground warrens. Examples can be viewed at the Imperial War Museum in London and at many local museums in Belgium and France.

I have no idea if George ever experienced any of these bunkers – they are part of the many issues I wish that I was able to quiz him about. He certainly knew all about the trenches though and clearly hated everything about them.

Chapter Eleven

〰〰〰〰〰〰〰〰〰〰〰〰〰〰〰〰〰〰〰〰〰〰〰〰〰〰〰〰〰〰〰〰〰〰〰〰

Many other terms have served to confuse me about World War One throughout my life and untangling some of these have helped me inch towards a better understanding of circumstances that prevailed during that terrible period.

Not being a military man myself many of the terms used, I realised, meant nothing to me and simply became an obstacle to me understanding what I was told – or read. I realised, when talking to others, that these confusions applied to them as well. This lead to me researching a bit further as to what military terminology actually refers and what the various ranks of office mean. I suspect that it mattered little to George – he never made much reference to officers or to the various Army structures. He related to his 'old Corp' and so I felt a need to find out where they fitted in to the overall structure. Because

A very brief summary of the structure and military terminology attached to that – and which is commonly encountered when reading about the War – is now attempted.

Take the overall Army structure. Firstly, accept that our force was known as the 7th Army – some 300-400,000 men controlled by the Commander-in-Chief (from December 1915 Field Marshal Sir (later Earl) Douglas Haig).

This was split into a number of (five) Army Corps each of which was controlled by a Lieutenant General and comprised 75-80,000 men in each Corps.

A Corps was divided into (usually four) Divisions lead by a Major General with about 18,000 men in each. The Division was the main tactical unit in the British Army. In other words if a part of the Army was to deploy it was as a Division that it did so.

A Division was sub-divided into Brigades headed by a Brigadier General controlling about 4,000 men.

A Brigade comprised four Battalions of 1,000 men led by a Lieutenant Colonel. It was usual to have Battalions drawn from different Regiments to comprise a Brigade. The intention behind this was to balance specialisms held by different regiments and to minimise the social impact associated with excessive losses that might occur in battle.

A Battalion was divided into Companies of some 220 men under a Lieutenant Colonel with a Major as deputy, supported by those of Captain rank. (George was in the 2nd Battalion of the York & Lancaster Regiment.) Battalion HQ would have a Captain or Lieutenant – responsible for administration called the Adjutant – and another of the same rank as Quartermaster (in charge of supplies and transport).

usually numbered A to D and each company had those who undertook specific roles such as signallers, batmen (personal servants to officers), drummers, cooks etc. as well as specialist combatants like machine gunners or rifle bombers (which was what George was).

In each Platoon an NCO (Sergeant or Corporal) led a Section of 10-12 men. George's 'old corp' was almost certainly his Platoon leader.

A section would work together as a day-to-day 'unit' although this would have been continuously disrupted by losses, transfers, casualties and illness of individuals. A section is what the likes of an ordinary soldier, like George, would have most clearly related to for day-to-day soldiering. Sections would have their 'specialists' – George, as said, was a rifle bomber. There would have been snipers (about 25/Battalion), machine gunners (eventually about 96/Brigade – divided between heavy machine guns – Vickers – and lighter, more mobile, Lewis guns) and mortar bombers (these were also divided between heavy mortars capable of firing missiles weighing about 150lb over 1,000m, medium fired 35lb bombs about 500m and light (Stokes) trench mortars which infantry, rather than specialist gunners, would operate).

Records show that the majority of the actual fighting was carried out by the 'specialists' with many of the ordinary infantrymen going through a major action not having fired their guns at all. The specialists tended to display the more aggressive instinct too – although, possibly they were just obliged to do so.

It was only by attempting to understand this structure that I managed to get some sort of comprehension about these army terms which I – like many others – had 'read over' so many times when attempting to learn more about our illustrious fighting men.

Made Em Cry.indd   78

11/8/2012   1:39:32

be more effective in dealing with counter attacks. Many reckon that the grenade (for that is what a rifle bomber fired) was the equivalent of the throwing spear of medieval armies or bayonets at Waterloo all being used for fairly close quarter work. A rifle grenade – such as George was trained to use – had a rod attached and was fired for close quarters work by a blank cartridge. Many stories abound about the fear that combatants on each side had for grenades (the British hand thrown grenade was often called a Mills bomb). George's story about that fear, that I clearly recall, went like this:

We were caught just in front o' their bloody trenches when two or three o' them Jerries stood up. They'd only got trenching tools and we had only got woiorin' tools (he must have been referring to his being in a wiring party – I've no idea whether it was light or dark – but guess the latter as that is when most of this sort of work took place – GB). *We just sort o' froze fer a moment staring at each other. Oi reckon oi yelled 'Watch out he's goin' fer his gun or somethin'' 'coz the old corp reached fer his pocket and threw somethin' – well thank god the old Jerries doived down and we scarpered – oi think we stopped in a shell hole or sap trench or somethin'. Then I realised there had been no bang. Old corp was a'larfin'. 'What happened?' oi asked. He got his breath back and said – 'Well, blast, that was moi tobacco tin – they thought oi had thrown a grenade at 'em'. Between gasping for air the rest of us began ter laugh too – but oi've often thought how bloody lucky we were – and how scared we all were – on both sides. Then o' course old Corp says 'C'mon lets have yer baccy so oi can have a ciggy'. Oi passed me old tin to him so he could roll his fag.*

The theory was that every man was trained to do their particular job – and George always reckoned that, later in the war when he went in, they were properly trained. But the stories that he

George's consciousness of going 'into the line' for the first time helps to give a little idea of what it was like – although no words are capable of recreating the full horror of life in that awful War. He was most reluctant to talk about the trenches but did recount some of his experience when he first went right to the front at Passchendaele east of Ypres. This would have been in April 1918 as the German Army launched its last offensive.

It is best to attempt a description of what 'the front' was like. Due to the heavy shelling any description attempted was likely to get disrupted at any moment. However, generally the reserve lines contained troops ready to move forward to join an attack or relieve troops in the front lines. In this area were the forward first aid posts, cooking facilities and the like. These tended to link to roads which allowed supplies and men to be moved forward from depots further back. A more detailed description of trenches and what was experienced in them is attempted in Chapter 14.

The Battalion that George had been assigned to, on arrival in France (The 2nd Battalion on the York & Lancaster Regiment) had been moved north after a terrible mauling in March (over 400 officers and men killed, wounded or missing in two days) when the Germans commenced their 'big push' in Picardy (The Somme). They were in reserve just east of Ypres in April 1918 when George joined his new colleagues. The regular reorganising of units and the difficulty in providing drafts of men to make up strength, necessitated by huge losses, meant that there was a severe disruption to the effectiveness of units as a result of unfamiliar arrangement of units. Not only that George and his colleagues were flung into a creaking defensive line which was already weakened by the reduction in the numbers of Battalions in a Division from 13 to 10 in addition to the British taking over about 15 miles of trenches north of Ypres towards Nieuport) with a numerically smaller Army than he had had at his disposal in 1917.

As mentioned earlier the Germans used fresh troops withdrawn from the Russian front and refined tactics in an attempt to drive the Allied forces back to the English Channel. In the first few days of April, George's battalion were ordered to the front line to help contain the German advance which commenced about a month after their advance further south. So the Brigade of which the 2nd York & Lancasters were part, faced the brunt of German pushes against the British-held front both to the south and in the north in the space of just one month. The new men, George amongst them, had no time to train and little chance to acclimatise to the terrible conditions. George's recall to me went something like this:

Corse we never even got ter the real front line that first toim we were moved up from reserve. Oi remember being ordered forrard and we crept along these damned trenches – half the duckboards were missing (duckboards were slatted wooden frames used to keep feet above the liquid mud along trenches – GB). *Every now and then yer would sink down ter yer knees in this stinking mud. The big guns were banging away on both sides – it were raining. Chaos rained too – yer daren't put yer head up – oi could hear bullets whistlin' and whoinin' away over the top of us. It was as much as yer could do to stay on yer blinkin' feet and yer were troin' ter move in a sort of crouch. Anyway – suddenly oi looked around and oi didn't recognise the blokes in front or behind me. Then there were loads of blokes coming in the opposite direction troyin' to get past us with staring eyes lookin' loik blinkin' madmen. Oi thought to meself 'this is no good – oim bloody lorst where's them blokes oi started off with?'*

81

was goin' on. Oi said to someone 'Oi don' know where oi should be – oi can't see them blokes oim sposed ter be with'. Someone shouted back that they hadn't seen anyone that they knew for a couple o' hours. Just as oi was startin' to panic a bit the old corp yells out ter me ter go with him – he had got stuck behind me and with all the chaos had only got one or two others of our lot with him. He found one of our officers who said somethin' about fallin' back and so we turned and stumbled our way back to some reserve lines which were choked with injured and dead men and people just stood in complete shock seemin' not ter be noticin' anythin' around 'em. The sky was black even though it was April the noise just about deafening. We spotted some more of our boys and an officer got us organised a bit and we were told to get into a trench and start to throw some soil up so we could hold the Germans there. We were told they were roit behoind us but oi hadn't seen one at that point. It was loik oi imagin' hell is loik – oi s'pose oi shall foind out one o' these days!

◇◇

It was never possible to get him to talk much more about that sort of thing – it was only possible to get stories of certain incidents – such as those that have been recalled earlier – from him. What it is possible to say is that the 2nd York & Lancasters did fall back – as mentioned earlier – and George and his mates ended up near Zillebeke Lake on the outskirts of Ypres and the Battalion battle orders show that they were the main occupiers of the line that eventually halted the German advance in that sector – the map on page 100 gives some idea of their likely disposition according to the Regimental Battle Orders for that period. It was there that George performed his first sniper's

82

Zillebeke Lake and the Ypres-Commines Canal – sharing duties, as they were to do again later when moved to The Somme, with the King's Shropshire Light Infantry (KSLI) and The Buffs who constituted the other members of the Brigade.

At first this constant bombardment *'nearly drove yer crackers'* but gradually the German offensive lost momentum and petered out although George reckoned that there were never any days, over the next few weeks or so, when shells did not land somewhere *'too damned close'*. Just trying to imagine this makes me feel stressed and – I have to admit – frightened. Having stood somewhere close to the likely spot near Zillebeke Lake (see Images pages 104 and 105) it is just about possible for me to begin to imagine how terrible it must have been for those who were involved – but not to allow how I might have coped with it. No wonder that George – and many like him – waited until near the end of their days before they 'opened up' and attempted some recall of their experiences for later generations. The memories were still too raw – and dreadful – to permit him, and them, to talk about them.

Many former servicemen hold great affection for the Regiment in which they served. George never spoke much about the York & Lancasters to me – and I never specifically asked him. I think that it is entirely understandable if he felt little close affection for or affiliation to the Regiment in which he fought because, after all, he was simply dropped into it and whisked off to an ailing front line as soon as he arrived in Belgium. He had no opportunity to develop any sort of attachment to the Regiment unlike those who joined during peacetime and were trained up with the units with which they served. The photographs of George taken when he was on leave in 1919 clearly show his shoulder strips for the others – he was.

CHAPTER TWELVE

I referred earlier to the ability that George had as a shot and that
he had carried off prizes for marksmanship during World War
Two when in the Home Guard. And that he had claimed that he
was unable to recall whether he had killed anyone when in the
Army in the Great War when I naively asked him about that when
a young boy.

One evening we were enjoying 'a glass' sat in our home and
my wife was out. I cannot now recall what might have prompted
him but suddenly he leaned back in the chair – fag in mouth as
ever – and started:

*Well- no oi-er… … corse when we'd finished training they realised
oi could hit most anythin' so they gave the snoipers flash at first but
then they changed me to a roifle bomber. Not long after we got out*

Jerry kept popping a few rounds our way and our officer called for 'Snoiper'. God knows what had happened to ours in all that chaos – so moi old corp told me to report.

The officer told me to get behind a slight rise in the ground where there was a dead 'oss sticking up and try to 'Keep their ruddy heads down so we can get sorted out down here'. Sounded like a bit o' sport, oi thought, and better th'n digging blasted trenches.

So oi got meself settled down and worked out how best oi could see without bein' seen. Well their trenches opposite us had this bit of a kink in one of 'em and oi could almost see straight down one length. Oi could see old Jerry as plain as day movin' around and letting a few pot shots off at my mates.

Well – oi soon had a few o' them – easier than hitting blinkin' rabbits it were.

◇◇◇

I interrupted and asked 'Do you mean that you killed some?'

Blast yes – couldn't miss. Now, o' course, oi don't feel so good about it but they were trying to hit us after all so oi just dropped 'em – a decent few oi should say. Oi kidded meself oi was a shot that was what oi was s'posed to do – or so oi thought.

Oi soon blasted learned though didn't oi? Y'see – 'cause oi had got several of 'em they worked out where they shots must be a' comin' from and soon after they turned the bloody artillery on my hoid'n' place.

Cor – oi were back and out o' that blasted place as quick as oi could move and they hit the ruddy thing too. It were a bit hot for a time – we all had to get our heads down for while.

nuisance – but oi took care never to draw too much attention to m'self after that first toim.

This event probably happened in April 1918. At this time the Germans had arranged armistice with Russia and had moved many trained, fresh troops to the western front and were starting their 'big push for the Channel'. During 1916–17 the Allies had moved the Germans back a few miles in the sector where George and his Regiment were now in the front line – near Ypres – but only at huge cost of life. Some of the gains further south in Picardy (generally called The Somme) were quite significant but in the north they only reached east to a ridge near to the village of Passchendaele a few miles east of Ypres. George's new Battalion should have joined the front line there to try to hold the German 'push' on 4th April 1918 but were never to get to their allotted trench position – it being overrun as they arrived (see Chapter 11). The above story probably relates to the time that they were trying to uprate reserve trenches near Zillebeke Lake that they had fallen back to when the Germans already occupied what had recently been British front line trenches. Standing by Zillebeke Lake on the outskirts of Ypres today it would take less than 30 minutes to walk to the town and, from where the Menin Gate can now be seen from outside the town, is close to the recorded disposition of the 2nd York & Lancaster Regiment in April and May 1918 – again the map on pages 98 to 99 gives some idea of the layout of that locality.

Given that George had only been with the 2nd York & Lancasters for a very short time when this occurred I am now surprised that 'his old corp' already knew that George was a good shot – clearly as they tried to stem the German advance over the preceding days George had showed his proficiency with a rifle – and that

We continued speaking – or at least George did for a while – I remember the light beginning to fade but left the electric light off so as not to break the spell of George's recall – and we chatted on about that experience. He clearly did not want to talk about the trenches too much but went on to recount:

Course – the boot was sometimes on the other foot. Oi 'member early one morning – a Sunday it was – oi had just been stood down from guard duty in the trench and thought oi would have a crap before troin' to get some sleep. As oi made me way to the reserve trench oi passed a bit of an old church yard and thought that would be a good place to 'leave it', y'know?

Oi had a bit of a squint around me and it seemed quiet. So oi, lent me roifle agin a wall, got down with me back against a gravestone and dropped me trousers and bent down. With that – bloody old Jerry fires and hits the other side of the gravestone. Cor – oi had me trousers up grabbed me roifle and was over that damned wall a'fore he let another one go!

(Laughing) Old Jerry had a sense o' humour – he didn't intend ter get me oi reckon – 'cause he must o' seen me go inter the graveyard ter start with and could ha' given me one then. He just thought he'd put the wind up an' watch me dance a bit. And oi did! Quite put me off having a crap that did!

◇◇◇

We did talk a bit about sleeping and he said that it was just never a problem for him. I asked about the noise of the guns, the wet, the lice – the awfulness that I had read about many, many times:

Y'just got used to it. Most o' the toim you were so damned toired y'oud just fall asleep wherever you were. Tell the trooth – yer'd fall soon have yer on a charge if they caught yer dozing off – and it was easy ter do.

When there was a big 'do' on yer'd p'raps not get any proper sleep or be stood down fer several days – cor it was mayhem on them occasions. Just loik a nightmare – noise – confusion – blokes getting blown t'bits. Never knew when o' them damned shells had your name on it.

Then if yer did get a few minutes yer were filthy and lousy and cold. Still – no good moaning – yer were there and had to put up with it. Some of 'em cracked up a bit – y'know tears and all that – shakin' all over. Oi just tried to shut it out – think o' the girls at the dances back home – wonder what my mates at home moit be up to and that sort o' thing – what they'd be up to on the farm and all that.

Even when yer weren't actually in the foir trench yer had things ter do. Loik – usually at noit – yer would have ter carry ammo and stuff up ter them that were in the front loin and there were flares – oo! Oi hated them damn things – and guns a goin'. Old Jerry got ter know where our roads were and it was nuthin ter get killed when yer were carryin' stuff to them poor beggars up front. Many did too.

Most of the blokes were good sorts – oi got matey with my corporal from about m'first day out there he seemed ter think oi was all roit. From Yorkshire somewhere he was – and we sort o' looked arter each other. If he had ter go and fetch wounded men in from in front of the trenches or put some woir up oi allus went with him and that sort o' thing. Any nasty job he was told ter do oi just went with him – gave each other good luck, we reckoned. S'pose oi was too young and too green ter know any different.

Not sure why – but old corp' and me hit it off from the start. He were older than me by a good bit but maybe 'cause oi tried not ter moan and just got on with it he sort o' took ter me.

89

Tell the trooth oi found oi couldn't bloody-well walk.

Corse he'd got to know me well by then he knew oi'd got a proper problem and he got the medics ter look at me a bit quick – good job it'd been a pretty quiet noit otherwise they'd 'a been maybe too busy t'bother with me.

They took one look – and said 'Trench fever'. Old corp laughed and told me oi were a 'Bloody skoiver' but made sure that oi were looked after. They got me back with the wounded ter the first aid place.

Oi was back in a week or two later – 'You needn't think you are going to miss any of the fun' I remember the doctor saying to me. Fun – huh! Anyway oi wanted to get back anyhow – no good t'me loiin about doin' nuthen'.

Oi soon looked up me old corporal and he wanted to know how oi'd got on with the nurses. Oi told him that oi was still too tender to think about that – he said he couldn't 'magine ever not thinking about a woman. Course normally oi would have had to agree with him at that point o' me loif.

Oh! oi was a bit steady for a week or two but when you have ter survive and keep y'self sharp ter what is going on around you y'soon forget about old aches n' pains. Still oi reckon oi went back too soon as oi were soon back in hospital. They took me t'Boulogne that toim. Oi gradually got better arter that – although the weather did begin to droi up a little and my lot had got moved.

I was keen to hear more of his experiences and took him out for a pint the next evening. Again the pub was a quiet bar and I tried to start him going again. Am I pleased that I did because he recounted one of the most extraordinary experiences that I can recall anyone sharing with me and it stays so vividly in my mind today. It would have been in the summer of 1918 in Picardy when foitin 'em off as they tried to stop us breakin' through – we'd managed to come through it all somehow o' other.

Anyhow – they eventually stood us down and we trooped back to get some sleep. The noise was still tremendous and there were people dashing everywhere behind the lines – munitions, guns, men, food, wounded all moving or being moved. Cor y'erve no idea – nor do yer want to have – what it's loik in a major 'do' – total madness.

We walked back about two moil oi reckon when we came into a farmyard. It wasn't too badly knocked about, considerin'. Things were movin reasonably fast boi that time so some buildings and that were still stood – not loik up at Woipers – nuthin left round there. Ennyhow – oi should say it were about evening when we got there and maybe it would have been in September toim o' year. One of the blokes saw this cart shed – it was stone-built and had a wooden floor for the loft over where they stood the carts. He went up the ladder to the loft and called down 'This is it boys – the floor's covered with hay – we'll be all roit up here'.

Oi 'member we stood our roifles together, took off our webbing and boots and putties and were soon asleep. We started to come round the next day – the usual farting and moaning and goin' ahead – one of em' went out for a pee and come back to tell us what a wonderful morning it was out there – warm and sunny. Guns still goin' loik mad o' course.

As we began to pull ourselves together several of us sniffed at an odd, yet somehow or other, familiar sort o' smell. 'Ventually someone kicked some of the hay that was spread over the loft – and that we'd slept on – asoide. There on the floor of the loft were the bodies of 18 Germans – we'd slept the noit on top of 'em!

When we got ourselves together and got downstairs out of the loft we looked up at the wooden floor and it was plain that some of our lot

The horror of that experience still lives with me as vividly today as when George recounted it to me and I wonder how I might now react if invited to sleep in a barn, in which hay or straw had been stored, given the impact that this particular tale has always had upon me! Furthermore, it simply amazes me that this group of young men were simply so physically shattered that they could drop to sleep so easily. Also that they had become so conditioned to the stench of the dead that they did not recognise the stink when entering the loft! I reflect, as others must too, on those periods in my life when I have been bored 'silly' by having to undertake some boring and irksome task for days on end. On re-reading George's recollections above I realise just how puerile my reactions have been when these men had become so inured to simply dreadful circumstances that it never occurred to them that this was something 'different' or exceptional to what they were seeing, hearing and smelling all the time at the front line – or just behind it in this case. It is frightening to realise what the appalling circumstances they were expected to contend with and I feel humbled by their experience.

CHAPTER THIRTEEN

◇◇◇

The 2nd Battalion York & Lancaster were gradually relieved from around Zillebeke and, as part of the then 6th Division began movement back southwards to The Somme from mid-May 1918 – George would have been with them at the start – the maps on pages 98, 99 and 100 may help readers to understand where these two zones are located. For a while they were holding the front line where the French and British Armies joined and some of the first American troops were attached to the Battalion to acclimatise to trench duties for a while.

As it routinely occurred, when action allowed it, when George's Battalion was relieved front line duties they withdrew for training and musketry practice – the 2nd York & Lancasters had about three weeks of this in June that year and during this period George was suffering from so called 'trench fever' which he had obviously scratching of the irritation that allowed their faeces to be worked into the skin and, eventually, the blood stream. Many who suffered this condition never returned to front line service but George was determined to do so – perhaps too determined for his own good as circumstances were to reveal (see Chapter 12). He told me how much he hated *'bein' cooped up'* and tried several times to be released back to his Battalion before persuading the medics he was fit again for duty on 30th July and then he did return to active duty. This was typical of the 'hard' man that I recall from my boyhood.

By now the German 1918 spring offensive (sometimes called The Third Battle of The Somme) had stalled due to difficulty in supplying it fully and general exhaustion. Although it had appeared as if Paris might fall at one stage the resolution of those poor, brave Allied soldiers eventually halted the Germans in Picardy which had reached as far west as Albert, which is north east of Paris, and Chateau Thierry – which is almost due east of the capital – again a quick check on the maps on pages 98, 99 and 100, may assist understanding of the geography.

The war was now to move into its final phase all along its front. The Germans had proved much better than the British at preparing strongpoints in the rear of their front lines. It can be assumed that attempting to take these – and with the continual artillery bombardments and rearguard actions and mines and booby-traps that would have been encountered – that the Allies suffered continuously as the German Army fell back. Although different from the swamp conditions, experienced in the trenches – particularly to the north – these more mobile days brought continued, if different, danger to those involved.

However, by July, thanks initially to some inspired actions by Australian troops, the battle in Picardy had changed and now

Somme River - as shown on the maps on pages 98, 99 and 100, again.

During this period of July and August the 6th Division – of which 2nd York & Lancaster were then part – were involved in a mixture of front line pursuit and rest/training. George's original keenness to return to his Regiment was premature as, just a week after returning to his duties he was once again admitted to hospital (7th Canadian Field Hospital at Etaples near Le Touquet on the Channel coast – see map on pages 98 and 99) and did not return to his Battalion until 8th October. This helps to account for his survival when so many others perished or were mutilated at this time. He was unfortunate to contract 'trench fever' but lucky that this withdrew him from immediate front line duties although his regiment were out of the front line for part of that time re-training in any case. (Several of the 2nd York & Lancasters have their graves in St Souplet Military Cemetery and were all killed between 24th – 27th September 1918 – they were relieved in the front line on 29th having breached the Hindenburg Line that day – just prior to George returning.) By the time that he was fully fit once again the Germans were in full retreat and daily advances by the Allies began to be the daily norm. The 2nd York & Lancasters had been heavily involved in the breaching of the Hindenburg Line but this was accompanied by serious losses in that assault (six officers killed or wounded and 210 other ranks killed, wounded or missing on 18th September alone, in preparation for the assault on the Hindenburg Line) in advancing almost two miles on that day.

The fact that the war was now more mobile and the Allies were advancing cannot conceal the horrors of that period though. It is clear today when walking these fields that the of five – cemeteries from the one that you may be standing in) shows how determined the German resistance to the Allied advance was. The graves – with the dates of the deaths shown on the immaculately preserved headstones – illustrate just how deadly the war continued to be even in these late stages. When stood in that part of the Communal Cemetery in the village of Ors – which contains a Commonwealth War Graves section – as late as 4th November 1918 (just one week prior to the Armistice which ended formal hostilities) 61 officers and men were killed in a single action. Two of the high ranking officers in that cemetery killed that day held the Victoria Cross and Military Crosses and 60 ranks of the Manchester Regiment perished – plus one from 2nd York & Lancasters – so George had been very close to the action again at that point. There has been noted in war records that very severe fighting in crossing the canal at Ors was experienced and it may have been this action in which so many – including decorated war heroes – perished. Although the Allies were now in the ascendancy not only the Commonwealth War Graves but the huge numbers of citations for bravery listed during those days are graphic illustrations of just how dangerous being in that theatre was.

George almost certainly was involved in the next major assault by the 6th Division on 8th October 1918 with an attack east of St Quentin towards Mericourt village which is situated on a ridge overlooking a dry valley up which the Division had to advance. The Divisional Commander decided to use the ridge north and south of this valley for the advance and the 2nd York & Lancasters were able to form a defensive line on the southernmost side to enable the 6th Division to maintain fighting contact with the French forces to its south. This action again brought losses to the

Made Em Cry.indd 96

11/8/2012 1:39:33

Everybody's favourite Uncle – taken outside the cottage where he spent the last 50 years of his life and where the author spent carefree school holidays and first remembered George.

Some of the many gravestones pictured in a Commonwealth War Grave near Mericourt in the Somme area. It is possible that George would have known these men, which highlights the deadly randomness of death in World War One.

97

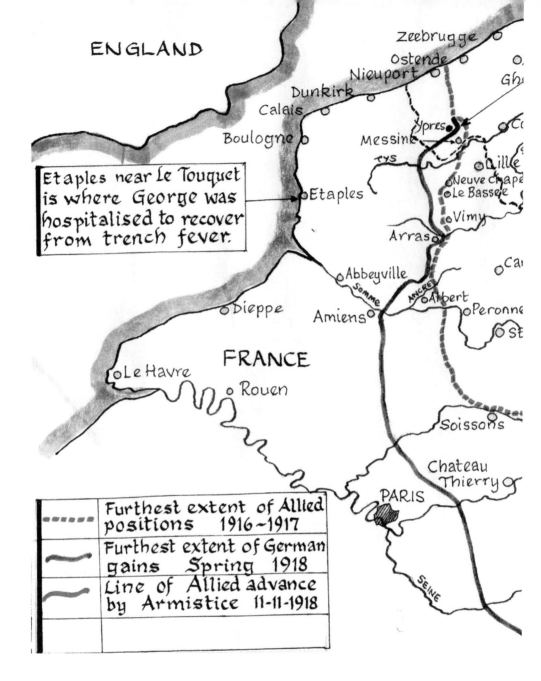

ENGLAND

Zeebrugge
Ostende
Nieuport
Dunkirk
Calais
Boulogne
Ghe
Ypres
Messine
TYS
Lille
Neuve Chape
Le Bassee
Vimy
Arras

Etaples near Le Touquet is where George was hospitalised to recover from trench fever.

Etaples

Abbeyville
Somme
ANCRE
Albert
Peronne
St

Dieppe
Amiens
Ca

FRANCE

Le Havre
Rouen

Soissons

Chateau Thierry

PARIS

SEINE

-----	Furthest extent of Allied positions 1916~1917
～	Furthest extent of German gains Spring 1918
～	Line of Allied advance by Armistice 11-11-1918

Made Em Cry.indd 98   11/8/2012 1:39:36

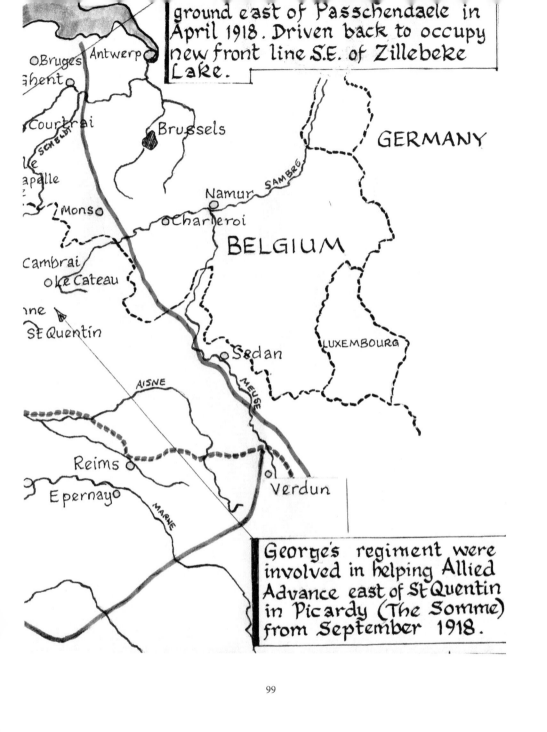

ground east of Passchendaele in April 1918. Driven back to occupy new front line S.E. of Zillebeke Lake.

George's regiment were involved in helping Allied Advance east of St Quentin in Picardy (The Somme) from September 1918.

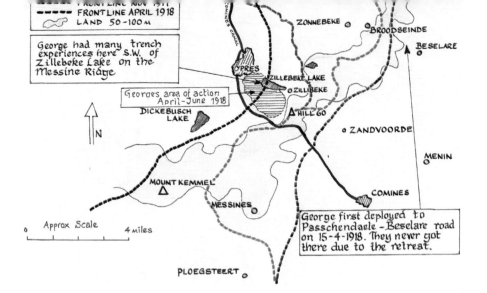

FRONT LINE NOV 1917
FRONT LINE APRIL 1918
LAND 50-100 M

George had many trench experiences here S.W. of Zillebeke Lake on the Messine Ridge

George's area of action April-June 1918

George first deployed to Passchendaele - Besclare road on 15-4-1918. They never got there due to the retreat.

ZONNEBEKE
BROODSEINDE
BESELARE
YPRES
ZILLEBEKE LAKE
ZILLEBEKE
DICKEBUSCH LAKE
HILL 60
ZANDVOORDE
MENIN
N
MOUNT KEMMEL
COMINES
Approx Scale
0   4 miles
MESSINES
PLOEGSTEERT

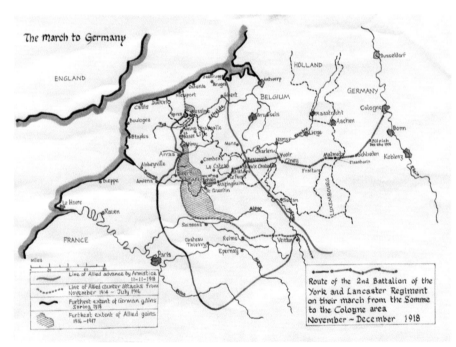

The march to Germany

ENGLAND
HOLLAND
GERMANY
BELGIUM
FRANCE
LUXEMBOURG

Line of Allied advance by Armistice 11-11-1918
Line of Allied counter attacks from November 1914 – July 1916
Furthest extent of German gains Spring 1918
Furthest extent of Allied gains 1916 -1917

Route of the 2nd Battalion of the York and Lancaster Regiment on their march from the Somme to the Cologne area
November - December 1918

100

...helped stem the German advance in 1918 and where he spent many a those weeks in the area between Zillebeke Lake and the Ypres-Commines Canal.

Left bottom: Showing the route taken by the 6th Division when deployed to Germany after the Armistice in 1918. It also shows the extent of German and Allied advances between 1914 and 1918.

Sir Edwin Lutyens' Memorial to the Missing of the Somme at Thiepval which is inscribed with the names of thousands of those lost in this theatre.

101

View today from the Paschendaele-Beselaere ridge in the area where George first went into action with the Yorks & Lancs Regiment on 13th April 1918.

Over the ground where so many lost their lives in the German spring offensive of 1918 in Flanders now stands Tyne Cot cemetery the largest Commonwealth War Grave anywhere in the world.

Remains of a German underground bunker cut into the chalky soil near Albert in Picardy (The Somme).

Distinct remnants of trenches still exist in many places – note the typical zig-zag arrangement used to minimise the effect of artillery blast.

Zillebeke Lake south-east of Ypres today. Deceptively peaceful compared to 1914–18 yet there seems to be a remarkable absence of wildlife visible.

The wonderfully restored Cloth Hall in the main square of Ypres today. When George passed through here in 1918 the whole town had been reduced to rubble by continuous artillery bombardment.

Mud is never very far away in Flanders. This view also shows how close Zillebeke Lake – where George spent three gruelling months in the trenches in 1918 – is to Ypres. The Germans were never able to take and hold the town.

An example of the remains of trenches in Picardy (Somme) area – note that the soil is chalky out of the river valleys – quite different from Flanders with its high water table and near-universal mud.

105

Two unknown fellow-sufferers of trench fever shown at the Canadian Military Hospital at Etaples on the Atlantic coast taken when George was also recovering from this debilitating condition there in 1918.

14 Platoon of the 2nd Battalion the York & Lancaster Regiment – of which George was a member – taken at their billet in a girls' school just outside Cologne in 1919. George is at the extreme left of the second row from the back.

Made Em Cry.indd   106

11/8/2012   1:40:00

George and his mates at Zulpich – the cook is well-dusted in flour. George (hatless) stands immediately behind him. Is that 'the old corp' at the extreme right of this group?

When stationed in Cologne the 2nd Battalion York & Lancasters formed part of the parade inspected by the French overall Commander of the Western Front – Marshal Foch – seen inspecting the parade mounted outside Cologne Cathedral.

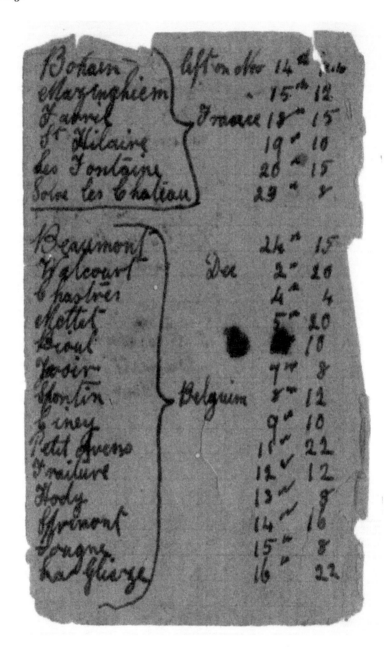

Place		Date	Miles
Bohain	left on Nov	14th	
Marzinghiem	"	15th	12
Fabril	France	18"	15
St Hilaire		19"	10
les Fontaine		20"	15
Solve les Chalian		23"	8
Beaumont		24"	15
Walcourt	Dec	2"	20
Chaslres		4"	4
Mottet		5"	20
Aroul			10
Tavoir		7"	8
Spontin	Belgium	8"	12
Ciney		9"	10
Petit Avens		10"	22
Tmailure		12"	12
Hody		13"	8
Sprimont		14"	16
Songne		15"	8
Radglierge		16"	22

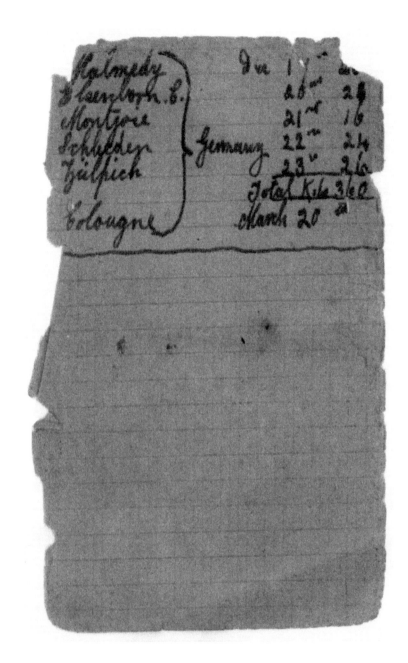

Malmedy
Elsenborn.B.
Montjoie
Schleiden
Zülpich

Cologne

Germany

Dec 17   20
26   24
21   16
22   24
23   26
Total Kils 360
March 20

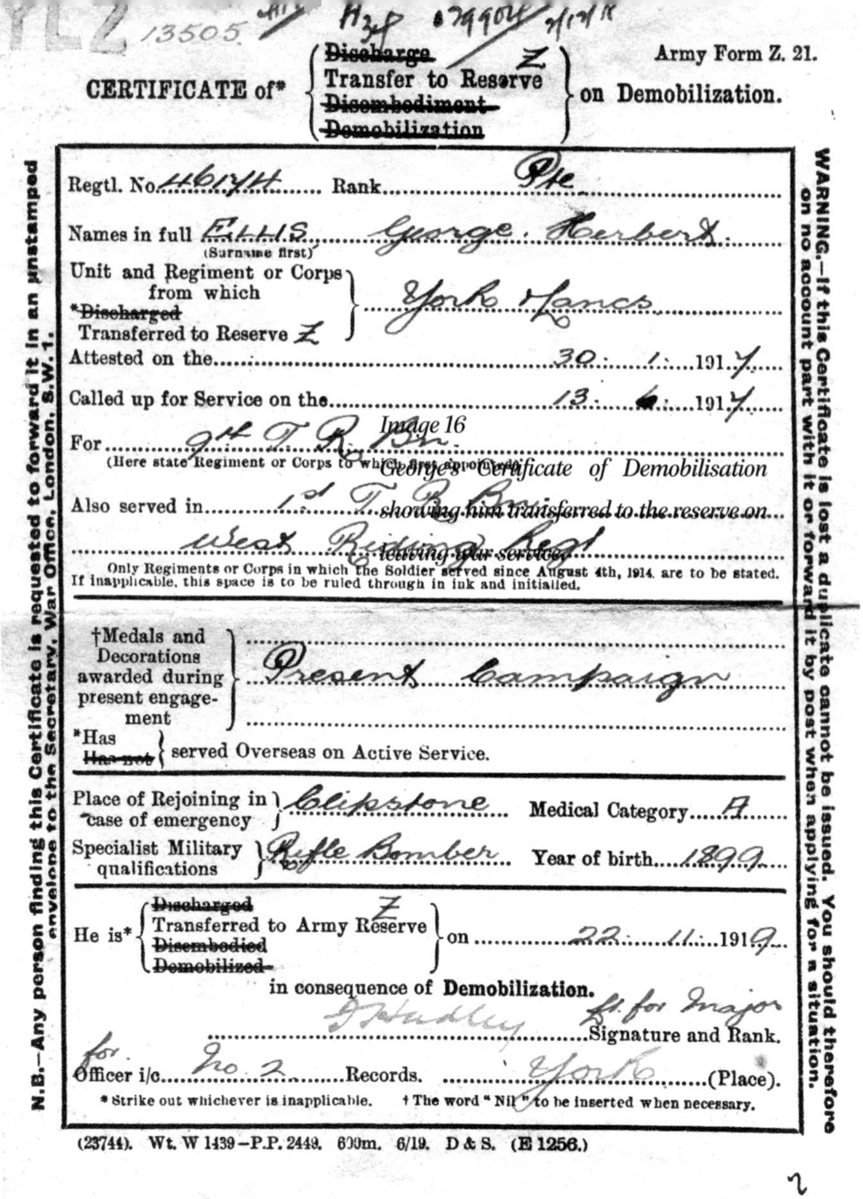

YLZ 13505 ... Hzp 79904

CERTIFICATE of* {
~~Discharge~~ Z
Transfer to Reserve
~~Disembodiment~~
~~Demobilization~~
} on Demobilization.

WARNING.—If this Certificate is lost a duplicate cannot be issued. You should therefore on no account part with it or forward it by post when applying for a situation.

N.B.—Any person finding this Certificate is requested to forward it in an unstamped envelope to the Secretary, War Office, London, S.W. 1.

Regtl. No. 46174 ... Rank ... Pte

Names in full *Fields* ... George Herbert
(Surname first)

Unit and Regiment or Corps
from which
*Discharged
Transferred to Reserve Z
} York & Lancs

Attested on the ... 30 . 1 . 1917

Called up for Service on the ... 13 . 6 . 1917

Image 16

For ... 9th T. R. Btn
(Here state Regiment or Corps to which the soldier belongs)

George's Certificate of Demobilisation

Also served in ... 1st T. R. Bn ... showing him transferred to the reserve on
West Riding Regt ... leaving war service

Only Regiments or Corps in which the Soldier served since August 4th, 1914, are to be stated. If inapplicable, this space is to be ruled through in ink and initialled.

†Medals and
Decorations
awarded during
present engage-
ment
} Present campaign

*Has
~~Has not~~ } served Overseas on Active Service.

Place of Rejoining in
case of emergency } Clipstone ... Medical Category ... A

Specialist Military
qualifications } Rifle Bomber ... Year of birth ... 1899

He is* {
~~Discharged~~
Transferred to Army Reserve Z
~~Disembodied~~
~~Demobilized~~
} on ... 22 . 11 . 1919

in consequence of **Demobilization**.

D Hadley ... ft. for Major
.... Signature and Rank.

for
Officer i/c ... No 2 ... Records. ... York ... (Place).

* Strike out whichever is inapplicable.   † The word "Nil" to be inserted when necessary.

(23744). Wt. W 1439—P.P. 2449. 600m. 6/19. D & S. (E 1256.)

110

George, the dashing young beau, posing for a snapshot in his home village of Ridgewell in North Essex when home on leave in 1919.

Picardy, with its rolling fields, appears peaceful now but when George was near here in 1918 it was like 'hell on earth'. Near Fresnoy-le-Grand.

– to imagine the stress and fatigue the troops must have been under at that point. Imagine that and then try to feel how they might have done when ordered to then march two miles north to relieve Americans and hand over a commensurate length of line to the French on their right – well, that is what they actually did under the cover of darkness! On top of that many of them attacked again the next day to take the small town of Bohain which was found to contain a large store of German materials.

After a few days in reserve the 6th Division was moved further north again along the front and were successful in helping to drive the Germans out of some ground where they had been fiercely resisting the advance and they then managed to hold the ground that they had taken.

So the pattern was now developing. Take German-held trench positions – resist counter-attacks – occupy – be relieved and stand down in reserve ready for the next wave.

Over this period from late September – including when George rejoined his Battalion – they had marched some 50 miles and captured over 300 pieces of artillery and almost 17,000 prisoners. By 9th November 1918 a full German retreat was underway almost everywhere along the entire front from Flanders in the north to the Swiss border. On 11th November, when the Armistice was signed, the 6th Division was out of the front line being billeted in and around the town of Bohain (shown on the map on page 11) that it had helped to relieve a few weeks earlier. Perversely I found this town the least attractive of those visited in this immediate area today – but it must have seemed bliss to the men who were there at that time that the odds against their maiming, death or capture were markedly lengthened so, no matter the impression I gained getting on for

de Em Cry.indd   113

11/8/2012   1:40:06 PM

countryside found around Marlborough in Hampshire/Wiltshire with gently rolling chalk downland. Today the area is not unattractive but is featureless with few trees, no hedges and, a resulting, lack/absence of bird life. Some of this lack of trees must result from the effect of continual shelling during the battles that raged over the area and the legacy of that war continues today with several agricultural workers each year dying when their machinery strikes previously concealed, unexploded munitions.

I was able to use the Operational Orders for the 2nd York & Lancaster Regiment to guide me where to look for where George and his colleagues might have been across this area of The Somme front in those terrible days of Autumn 1918. What was simply awful to me was that I had the proof needed that they had 'passed that way' because every village mentioned in those Orders contained either a Commonwealth War Grave or an area within their own municipal cemeteries set aside for the war dead. In every village/ town referred to in those archives, graves to men of the Y&L appeared. The sheer randomness of death has quite an impact on the mind of anyone who stands to ponder such circumstances. George's Battalion Commander at this stage was Lieutenant Colonel J.R. Robertson and the Orders were issued in his name. Their major offensive in the area of Mericourt/Fontaine-Uterte villages was tricky as they had to maintain contact with the 47th French Division on their right – as they attacked – and the British 16th Infantry Brigade on their left. Whippet Tanks were used and the whole attack commenced under a creeping barrage – this is where artillery laid down heavy fire which moved in front of the attackers towards the enemy lines in an attempt to disrupt the defences. They were to form defensive positions to ensure that they could support other Battalions in the attack and prevent any and formed the second wave in the advance which was successful in taking and holding the high ground between Mericourt and Beauregard and maintaining essential contact with the French to their right.

In these Battle orders each Company within the Y&L had their own dispositions and functions detailed and, as mentioned, this particular action was successful – although deadly for many as evidenced by the presence in the various cemeteries of the headstones commemorating those from the Y&L Regiment and the others involved. The terrible encounters to cross the Ors Canal – when so many men died just a few days prior to the Armistice – is detailed in orders issued in late October. The York & Lancasters were one of the units involved to clear the town of the enemy in preparation for the assault to cross the Canal – one can only imagine the tension that would have arisen given this order with the risks to life that it would have held. The quiet cross roads on near deserted country lanes – as they now are – assumed important strategic purpose in 1918 and it difficult to imagine the deadly nature of them nearly a century later. For instance holding the line on the Malgarni-Bazuel road (still a tiny narrow country lane today) was clearly expected to be a test for the Battalion and of importance to the pending action to cross the nearby Canal. Today it is just a quiet rural backwater – albeit with Commonwealth War Graves which are clearly visible dotted all over this rural scene.

To stand in areas east of villages/towns like Mericourt and Bohain today – where George might well have stood under very different circumstances in 1918 – generated an emotional response in me that I have never experienced anywhere else. I feel a kind of embarrassment – guilt almost – that all these men to help retain the kind of society that we enjoy today. I also experienced feelings of acute pain – and anger even when – stood in packed crowds at the Menin Gate in Ypres at the 8pm last post – which is still celebrated every single day of the year – when a group of young Germans laughed, talked and attempted to wave a German flag during the act of remembrance. If they wanted to cause distress they succeeded, without doubt. A number of those present – from many different countries – shed their tears. Whether those were cast as a reaction to the tasteless, moronic behaviour of a few or to the memory of those whose lives were being commemorated I am not entirely sure – on that occasion it could have easily been both when, I know, it should have only been the latter. It served to reinforce the necessity of continuing to remember these terrible wars and those who sacrificed their lives and those who gave so much of their youth to support their nation's way of life and to protect such memories lest the attitude of the few – who would desecrate such service through mindless behaviour today – might prevail.

CHAPTER FOURTEEN

<><><><><><><><><><><><><><><><><><><><><><><><><><><><><><><><><><><><><><>

As previous parts of the text have emphasised – I attempted on numerous occasions to get George to explain more to me – I still regret not being more persistent but it seemed hardly fair to do so – especially as I now know he never spoke of those few years to anyone else.

I wanted to try to understand what a day in those dreadful trenches – which caused him to be so ill with pyaemia – were like. He told me some things which I have tried to report and, as a result, I know of the stink and noise and the wet – but still wonder just how ordinary young men were able to adapt to such alien circumstances?

I have studied numerous books, visited museums in Belgium, France and at home and stood in the remains of trenches all over Flanders and The Somme. But when people like me stand on are no shell holes full of water, body parts or decaying horses. How did these men live when all the things I cannot see were so real and apparent to them?

Just what was a day in those hell-like trenches in Flanders, in particular, like?

Protection for infantrymen started off in 1914 simply as rifle pits dug into the ground but these were soon to be joined together to form trenches. The impression of a complex of inter-connecting slits cut into the ground by hand (usually at night when the work might be better concealed) would describe the layout at the front if looked down upon from above. In fact, around Ypres (where George first experienced fighting) the low lying, sodden land, previously described, meant that most trenches in that area were mainly above ground level with breastworks being thrown up and using sandbags and reinforcing materials to offer protection.

Nearest the enemy – and the distance between their comparable lines and yours might be anything from 30 yards to a thousand – were the true front line trenches. These were better dug and deeper than those behind with, hopefully, a better parapet to protect the occupants from direct fire. In some, trench walls may have some abutments or dugouts below which officers might cover (other ranks generally had to make use of whatever they could for cover) from shrapnel. From these front or forward trenches into the gap between your line and the enemy ('no man's land') might be dug some, so called, sap trenches which might protrude some 20-30 yards to allow checks on activity in the lines opposite to be monitored.

'No man's land' would probably have been seen as a morass in which many shell holes were seen through a maze of barbed wire. This was a constant part of life in the trenches. This wire

wire – narrow routes, through which those knowing the layout, might creep to undertake observation of the enemy or even carry out a night time raid on the trenches opposite. All the work of laying or replenishing wire was conducted at night with those carrying out the work trained to 'freeze' or dive into shell holes whenever flares were sent up – see George's experience of this kind of activity which is recounted in Chapter 11.

The front line trenches were usually actually two lines of trenches about 20 yards apart and joined by a number of communication trenches or 'alleys'. The foremost trench was the 'fire trench' often with steps cut into the front wall for those on duty to stand. About 20 yards behind and parallel to the fire trench was the 'command trench'. This is where officers were often to be found in covered dugouts along with the necessary paperwork. The command trench would offer better cover for those troops not actually on duty at that moment and this was where the latrines were typically found.

Behind the front two rows of trenches – probably some 70-100 yards back – would have been the second line or reserve trenches in which resting or fresh troops might stand ready to support an assault and/or which would be used to fall back to in the case of a faltering defence if the front line were taken. George reckoned that it was some officers' idea of relaxation and rest to have you digging new or improving old trenches or filling sandbags when you actually stood down from frontline duties – *'Not moi idea of a day orf! Anyhow – when yer were doing that sort o' thing yer could still get killed'* he told me.

Behind this second row was, typically, a third row of trenches-again up to about 200 yards distant and – depending upon local circumstances – where troops in reserve might be dug in. Then and were called communication trenches. Troops would typically exchange with those in front/behind every eight days on a 'quiet' front – in practice this usually meant two Battalions on front lines swapping with two that had been in reserve.

All rows of trenches tended to zig zag rather than run straight – as they had at the start of the war – to reduce the numbers of maimings and deaths when a direct artillery hit on them occurred. Their exact disposition depended upon the topography of the ground and, to some extent, the position of the enemy lines.

Sometimes the line of the trenches protruded in to 'no man's land' from the frontline – these were known as a salient. George told me that a salient was *'Where yer got shot at from the sides as well as the front – we hated them bloody things – yer had to keep yer heads down all the damned toim'*.

The trench walls were probably reinforced with sheets of corrugated iron and timber. Most work on these had to be undertaken at night due to the risks of being observed during daylight hours. George once said *'Even the trenches could kill yer – if one o' them damned shells knocked in a wall yer could be buried aloiv when the walls collapsed'*. As he explained – and records show – there were any number of ways of losing your life in World War One.

The bottoms of the trenches may have been lined by duckboards (often termed 'banana skins' by some due to the way that they tended to became slippery). These were timber slats nailed to a timber frame and it was usual – particularly in Flanders – to be given one of these to carry – in addition to normal kit – when moving up from the reserve to front trenches.

Stirrup pumps were used to pump water out of the trenches. These were held in place by holding small plates beneath the feet hooded and much fought over low lying land those gave nothing more than a few hours of modest improvement in localised parts of a trench – but they helped to boost morale a little if comfort only marginally and temporarily.

To help assist safety – periscopes were increasingly used to monitor the enemy so that the need to put a head at risk was reduced. Even so some sharpshooter would succeed in 'taking these out' from time-to-time.

In the area between the lines of trenches would have been sited some heavily fortified (and camouflaged) 'strongpoints'. Typically these would have housed the heavy machine guns and, possibly a little further back, heavy mortars. These positions were almost always targets for artillery and this accounts for the very high ratio of losses among machine gunners in particular.

Records show that increasingly elaborate measures were taken to mask activities in front line trenches with artificial trees and the like being constructed to allow forward observation and even sniping to be better concealed from the other side as the war progressed. In fact the term 'camouflage' (from the French camuffare – to disguise/deceive) first came into use during World War One to describe some of the increasingly elaborate measures used to conceal intentions of one side from the other. This became even more necessary especially as aeroplanes became extensively used to aid gunnery officers to accurately identify their targets.

Behind all this were the areas that provided immediate support to those in the front line. First Aid posts, supply dumps and cookers (which were normally coal-fired) to provide the necessary support to those in, or about to be, action.

So it is your 'turn' to be in the front line and neither you, or those facing you, are planning a major attack today – how was the time spent?

to'. If considered 'clear' then there would be opportunity to cook, sleep, write or clean weapons – but always to endure the continuous gunfire. This then meant that you would have periods when you were on lookout or guard duty to make sure some surprise venture by the enemy did not take your stretch of the trench by surprise with turns 'stood down' in between. *'One of the really queer things was that the guns were gooin' ahead most o' the toim – terrible it was – but as soon as they stopped fer a bit – yer could hear birds a-twitterin' away'* George told me. Although he mentioned that writing home was one of the ways that troops spent any spare time he never wrote home. There were one or two examples of Field Service Postcards that he sent to his parents but these had no messages on them he just let them know that he was still alive *'Oi never was – nor have been – one fer wroitin'* he stressed.

At sunset the order to 'stand to' was given and then working parties were detailed for certain duties. These groups might be required to mend wire or lay new sections in 'no man's land'. It was a time when dead or wounded could be brought back to the lines after an action. It could mean that a raiding party was ordered to go and find out what the enemy opposite were up to or to capture prisoners for interrogation or to capture their raiding parties. Although he never gave me any details, the fact that George said many times *'Oi allus teamed up with me old corp if he was up to somethin''* almost certainly means that he joined in that sort of activity. Would I have ever had the bravery to do so, I frequently wonder? YET – he always played down the fact that he did anything remotely brave – just like all those whose recollections of that time have come into the public domain either by their comments or the publication of their diaries. It

The standard sort of wear for the front line troops was a fairly rough, woollen khaki tunic (what we now tend to call a battledress top) over a collarless shirt and trousers with putties around the lower legs up to just below the knees. These were like canvas bandages which were meant to protect trousers and lower legs from the wet. Boots were heavy leather issue which came up over the ankle joint. Almost all the men wore braces and a belt to secure the trousers and thick shirts underneath. George reckoned that his shirts and tunics were *'rough old stuff and yer itched even before the loice got yer'*. The helmets were domed with a rim right around the lower edge and were held in place by a leather strap which passed under the chin and was joined to the internal leather head bracing. Helmets replaced the more comfortable soft caps worn at the start of the war as those gave inadequate protection against shrapnel. In addition canvas straps over the tunic held a series of pouches – which held personal belongings and essential items – and a haversack on the back and over this, usually with a single strap which went over one shoulder, was a separate bag which held a gas mask. In addition of course weapons had to be carried according to the individual's specialism – George's rifle as a rifle bomber – would have held the attachment for firing grenades which he may have hung from his webbing.

These descriptions gleaned from records and George's comments conceal some of the true horrors of such a life. The living conditions were inhuman – if you stayed alive. The constant shelling (over 720 million artillery shells and mortars were fired during hostilities) was everyone's nightmare bringing potential death at any moment – and it, all too frequently, did. And how impunity, the stinking wet, the clothes ridden with lice, the cold, the fear and the living with the loss of someone you had been talking to just a few moments before who could suddenly be blown into unrecognisable pieces. Those were the trenches and the reality of trench life. The fact that these stinking lines stretched from between Ostend and Dunkirk on the Belgian coast right across France to near the Swiss border south east of Verdun provided an extraordinary distance over which a multitude of opportunities for these horrors to be played out, night and day for four years, existed.

George always stressed that it was a terrible period even though he spent much less time at the front than many. He said once:

Yer felt as though yer didn't count fer nuthin' – so yer learned ter look out fer yerself – troid ter make sure yer stayed aloiv – old corp and oi sort o' looked out fer each other – troid ter watch each others back – that sort o' thing. It's queer how excoited and full o' adventure yer were to start off with but how soon yer just became numb to it all, 'Corse oi were better off than them poor old married blokes – oi felt sorry fer them – 'coz' they had kids and that back at home – oi only had meself ter look after'.

Although George did spend less time in Belgium and France than many, he was rarely ever out of the front line when he was there. Yes – there was a break for training before the advance through The Somme but a very high proportion of George's time was spent on true frontline duty. Certainly he was never in a 'cushy' sector of the line where nothing much was happening.

For extended periods of time an attitude of 'live and let live' prevailed between the protagonists which meant tacitly avoiding activities that would provoke large scale retaliation from the

Made Em Cry.indd   124

11/8/2012   1:40:07

stories of 'blind eyes' being turned to each other's patrols into 'no man's land'. This does not mean that raids did not take place to extract intelligence about opposing units in a sector or to destroy particularly damaging areas of trench. In some sectors – and during much of 1915–16 – there were really only local activities rather than continual large offensives with extended periods of generalised inertia in between. Raids were generally hated by the men although some Battalions on both sides were committed and aggressive 'raiders'. If they were well-planned and rehearsed, in order to achieve a specific objective, then they might be better tolerated by those called to undertake them. But where such activities were ordered 'from above' just to 'raise morale' (it usually had the opposite effect) they tended to be carried out half- heartedly by both officers and men in many cases.

It is very likely this attitude contributed to the post-war attitude of 'bugger the toffs' which became so prevalent in society in general in the 1920s and 1930s – and even more noticeably after World War Two leading to a blurring of the distinctions between classes that we have today.

Chapter Fifteen

◇◇◇

I remember asking George one day about an old decorated pot tobacco pipe with fancy metal fittings that used to sit by the fireplace at his home. I believe that it is called a meerschaum in German. *'Oo! that ole thing. Got that when we were in Germany and brought it back as a sort o' memento o' bein' there.'*

I was surprised to hear that he had been in Germany itself as I assumed, at that stage, the soldiers were simply brought home when the dreadful fighting and killing stopped in November 1918.

Blast no! – i' fact for the last day or two afore the foitin' ended the silly devils went a bit mad and we fought over a few yards o' ground roit up to the end. Blinkin' daft it were – loads o' our boys got killed – fer nuthin'. They said they wanted to be able ter watch ole' Jerry withdraw ter make sure he hadn't booby trapped everythin' – course he'd already done that.

Noo – arter the Armistice we marched from the front to Germany – follered ole' Jerry home yer moit say. Fifteen odd miles a day we had

126

a fat lot left loin' around – still we coped and it were better than the trenches anyhow.

◇◇◇

His daughter Jane told me that she had a copy of a record that George had kept of their quite epic march from Picardy to Cologne. On one of our visits to her she had found it – along with photographs of her Dad and kindly let me copy them and these appear on the relevant pages. A copy of the route taken is shown – see map on page 100 and the hand written diary on pages 108 and 109.

Within a few days of the signing of the Armistice on 11th November 1918 the 6th Division (of which the 2nd York & Lancasters were part) was designated as one of those to form the new Army of Occupation in Germany. They left the Bohain area, where they had been billeted at the very end of the fighting, and began to march to Germany across France and northern Belgium. Firstly they moved north eastward with the whole Division gathering together at the small French town of Solre le Chateau. The march proper then commenced on 23rd November and George crossed the border into Germany on 13th December. The distances marched tended to be shortened for two main reasons – if they found a good place to billet they stopped earlier in the day and, increasingly, they had to pause while supplies reached them due to the lack of food found en route. They got to the Cologne area – to Zulpich south east of the city – just in time for Christmas. George's record of the march shows that, from Picardy, they marched north eastward to cross into Germany from Belgium near the town of Malmedy, which is south east of Liege, then via German towns and villages like Lager Elsenborn, Montjoie, Schlieden and Zulpich – all east of Aachen, for Christmas at Zulpich and cleaned up for a Church Parade held on Christmas Day. George's record (see pages 108 and 109) shows that they covered about 340km (213 miles) in 37 days arriving at Zulpich south east of Cologne on 23rd December. The map shown on page 100 shows the route that the 6th Division took as they moved from France across Belgium and into Germany as well as the general disposition of the front line and the major towns.

George stressed that there was very little food around and, although they were supposed to 'live off the land' as they marched it was clear that the retreating Germans had already taken most things and the French and Belgian countrysides were in a pretty poor state. He said that the reality was that they moved at about the speed that food could be brought up to them. He made reference to quite a lot of incidents which occurred during the march to Zulpich where gateways and some buildings had been mined so someone slipping into a field gateway for a pee or snatch a quick look in a roadside building could easily trip a wire and get blown to bits. 'Seemed koind'a sad when they'd got through the wust of it' – and who couldn't agree with his sentiments and flicker of sadness – obviously it had happened to someone he had got to know.

The Armies of Occupation, as they were called, supervised a radius of 30km around three major German cities – Mainz, Coblenz and Cologne. There were barricades in the streets to begin with but restrictions on the population were gradually relaxed. Although there were progressive reductions in the number of troops stationed there the final withdrawal did not take place until as late as 1929.

So – yet another – to me – amazing episode in the quiet man's life began to unfold – he was actually in Germany too. Almost no one

Made Em Cry.indd   128

11/8/2012   1:40:07

the troop dispositions in Germany after World War II but few have any idea that a more limited army of occupation existed after the first War. However, the 2nd York & Lancaster Regiment formed part of this Army of Occupation and George's Platoon – number 14 – were billeted in a girls' school – there is a good photograph of them there and this, too, can be seen on page 106.

George found it all pretty boring as all there was to do was some training, marching, games, ceremonial parades with an occasional route march round surrounding areas to 'fly the flag' (on 4th February 1918 they were marched from Zulpich through Bessenich, Sievernich, Disternich and Weiler and were back at their base by 12.45pm). They were also involved in competitions with other members of the Brigade and won a transport competition on 6th February and were second in a ceremonial guard event on 10th February 1919. All this was marking time and George found it pretty boring but he did manage to return home on leave for two weeks in March/April 1919 and again at the end of September before being transferred to the reserve (effectively de-mobilised) on 25th October 1919.

Time in Germany was spent drilling, training and attending an occasional lecture (one on 13th January being on 'Historical Subjects' and on 22nd January 1919 was entitled 'The Work of the Navy' – I have no indication of who delivered such talks or of the recipients' reactions to them). They also played football and some competitions between the constituent Regiments, comprising the 6th Division, were held. He also recalled boat trips on the River Rhine and visits to the zoo (he always believed that some of the empty cages were a result of a dreadfully hungry public eating some of the animals that had previously been caged there!). I also possess a photograph of troops lined up outside Cologne Cathedral while the French Marshal (Foch) inspects them – the assumption know the 'locals' in and around Cologne – which may be his way of saying that he did not enjoy much female 'company' during that period – I am sure that that would not have pleased him overmuch at the time – given his other stories about 'the ladies'. The fact was that fraternisation was banned – not that that would have stopped him – or his 'old corp' – from trying to get to know them given the other tales of that kind that he told me!

George recounted, from his time as part of the Occupation Forces around Cologne during 1919 and 1920:

Our lot had ter look after Cologne and we settled mainly at the edge of town and had ter look after things – loik police really. We was in what had been a girls' school. Course most of 'em didn't loik us bein' there. Oi can understand that as we were occupyin' forces and most o' them Jerries reckoned they hadn't lorst the war so we had no roit ter be there. In a way oi spose they were roit. It's no wonder them old Jerries didn't loik us bein' there. They always reckoned they never lost the war – only agreed to a ceasefire yet were being made to pay fer it and had land taken off 'em where Germans lived and they were now bein' made to live in another country. Corse they were damned near starvin' as well y'know – yer had ter feel a bit sorry for 'em. Most just had some o' that awful black bread ter eat fer a good whoil and they used to plead with us ter let 'em have some soap as they couldn't get hold o' any. Oi 'member that many o' them spoke a bit o' English – much more than we could speak German anyhow.

So much for the non-fraternisation policy that was supposed to have applied during that period!

I recall that this yarn was a bit slow in coming out but had learned not to push too hard as it used to often 'break the spell' of his reverie when I quizzed him too much. I decided to leave him to

Well! yes – oi-er... the thing was that a lot o' them Jerries had still got their weapons y'know. Yer could be walking down the street and suddenly someone would take a blinkin' pot shot at yer – froitened the loif out o' yer at toims. Oi wadn't used ter cities in them toims but there were a lot o' cobbled streets – quite woid too. I 'member that there were a lot of overhead woires fer trams so it wadn't too easy at all ter see old Jerry if he leaned out of a window to get a shot at yer. O' cause oi later got a bit of a look at London and that was about the same at that toim 'cept the roads weren't as woid as in Cologne – and there weren't people takin' a pot at yer...

I realised that this particular episode had quite an effect on George and – although he tried to make light of it – that is perhaps why it did not 'flow' as a reminiscence as when he recounted some of his other tales.

As mentioned, George did have some leave back home in Essex. He was at home for two weeks up to 4th April 1919 and again, for a similar period, between 16th September and 1st October. This accounts for the pictures that are shown of him looking very smart in a peaked Y&L hat and tunic complete with a 'swagger stick' (a polished cane). He would have had these taken during his periods of leave (See Preface and page 111).

During 1919 steps were gradually taken to return the 2nd Battalion to a regular army unit. Accordingly, any surviving volunteers who joined in 1914 and 1915 were demobilised and the ranks gradually filled with 'regulars'. This reorganisation led to George being transferred to the 1/4th Hallamshire Battalion of the York & Lancasters just before his first period of leave in March 1919.

army commitments ended on 31st March 1920 when the need for Class Z men on reserve was abolished. He was, from that point, fully back in 'civvy street' (a civilian). He would have been accorded The British War Medal which all those who served overseas were awarded and the Victory Medal – although these have not been located by his immediate family.

The time spent at relative ease after the end of formal fighting (being shot at and the lack of 'female comfort' aside) were about the easiest part of George's life before his eventual retirement. He said it was *'a bit of an adventure'* – to be overseas – *'with a lot o' young blokes loik yerself. Oi never would ha' got abroad if it hadn't been fer that War'* he said – and he never did leave the country again after 1919.

I wish so much now that I had thought to ask him more about it as several thoughts have occurred to me as I have thought back in the intervening years between listening and setting the stories down.

A major thought centres around his close wartime buddy 'the corporal' – whoever he was. George never made contact with him after he was 'demobbed' and returned to Essex – I asked him that once. I didn't go on to ask him why – and wish that I had done so.

They had been so close, did outrageous things together and had survived the madness and mayhem of Flanders and the Somme. Despite their age difference they were clearly extremely close – so why did they just walk away from each other, I have often wondered?

Maybe, of course it wasn't like that – perhaps the corporal went off somewhere else when George went to Cologne and they never had chance to make arrangements.

Although not too keen on recounting any experience usually, once he started, he went on to the end – typically finishing with something like *'Still – don't take no notice of a silly old bugger loik me…'*

Did something happen to the corporal after they had arrived in the Cologne area? Was this the reason George had some difficulty in completing his descriptions of this period? Is that why he had no contact with this bosom pal after he left the army? Was a booby-trapped gate or door or a sniper's bullet in the city the cause of the estrangement?

I did spot three names on the back of his march diary – they were 'Rifleman' though – no corporal mentioned – but I am pretty sure that he never contacted those either after he returned home.

Like I say I wish he was still here to ask now – and that I had thought to do so at the time. It haunts me that someone who he was clearly so attached to and spoke of with manly warmth should have just disappeared from George's consciousness. We know that the corporal survived the actual trench fighting because – see the opening of this book – George went with him to Paris before they marched off to Germany.

Being the tough nut that he was – if the corporal had been killed – I guess George would soon have taken a deeper than usual breath and got on with his life. Maybe they simply fell out over something like people can do. George was – after all and by his own admission – 'cussed' and they both were, after all, fond of the ladies…

CHAPTER SIXTEEN

◇◇

On demobilisation George returned to his home village of Ridgewell in North Essex. He lived with his parents and the – then – unmarried members of the family and worked on the land – at Bowles Farm (clearly the cause of the stackyard fire had not been discovered or was not mentioned and his involvement in the strike forgotten or forgiven). Old photographs of his home village of Ridgewell show a marked similarity around the village green and church area to how it appears today – except that the road now has a tarmac surface.

I wanted to find out as much as I was able about how he behaved in that period before he met my Auntie Beat and then got married. I attempted to find out what he had told people about his experiences in the War but that was to prove impossible.

I met up with George's one surviving brother – when I began my quest to fill in some 'blanks' on what he got up to after he likely to turn up 'in character' as a vicar, policeman or the like. Dressed up as such he would administer 'grace' prior to the meal, blessings thereafter if a 'cleric' and would 'book' those who he decided deserved to be classed as 'offenders' when in constable mode. He was a remarkable man travelling to the United States to meet up with a former American airman – who had been based at the village 'drome during World War Two and with whom he maintained a lifelong friendship – until over 90 years of age. He was a fixture in the village pub all his adult life and the organiser of any celebration that he could persuade people in the area should be held – the slightest pretext was enough for John.

Surely he would have a good fund of stories to help me understand how George settled down into country life again? When I sat down in the village pub with John he appeared a bit bemused when I attempted to quiz him about his older brother. He explained that George was a good bit older than himself – he was some 11 years older – so they never 'went around' together. He said that he recalled that George was a real laugh and never around the home that much as soon as work was over.

He did recount one very clear memory of George in that period though and this ties in very well with some of my recollections of George being able to 'fix' anything in ways that were not particularly 'conventional'. Apparently, as John recounted the tale, George had acquired an old bicycle when he came home and used it all the time – for work, to go to the pub or to the dances held in some of the neighbouring villages each Saturday. On one particular summer's evening George was all dressed up and ready to go off to a dance and, as he jumped on his bike, the tubular metal frame collapsed – it had rusted through and had 'given up the ghost' as John put it. George was determined that the centre of the tubular bike frame. He then pressed the other part of the frame over the opposite end of the branch – checked that it was a good fit – replaced the chain and pedalled off. John said – with a certain amount of admiration hardly lessened by the passage of 80 or so years – 'And, do you know, he rode that damned bike like that for ages after, too!'

John had very few direct memories of his brother though and felt that no one else was left in the village who would have known him. This bears out what I had discovered when talking to his daughters – he really did keep everything that he had experienced in the war to himself – he didn't even tell his brothers let alone his own family.

So I was left with the one story of that period that George had confessed to me. How he came about telling me about this happened like this. We had gone for a bit of a walk with the plan to skirt round the back of our village for a pint – it was a lovely summer's evening, I recall. I suggested that we use one of the footpaths in the village to make the walk a bit different and he thought that that was fine – so, off we went. As we left the pavement to go onto the footpath there were a lot of young saplings growing – mainly of elder which, as most people will know, gives off a very pungent and distinctive odour if the wood is broken when it is young. To ensure that George could get down onto the footpath without tripping over – he was well into his eighties by then and had already had a stroke (which he always brushed aside as 'a bit of a scare – that's all') I trod down some of these saplings and advised George not to let overhanging branches damage his eyes.

We negotiated this bank and the saplings safely enough and when we got onto the footpath proper he stopped and got his

Made Em Cry.indd   136

11/8/2012 1:40:07

'Vicar's wife, George – what are you on about you wicked old devil?' was the kind of response I made – and he laughed and continued:

Cor she was a lovely gal she was, boi! Best dancer for moils around too. She'd married this-here vicar – he was about twoice her age and o' course would never dream of goin' to a dance. But she wanted ter go every week. Y'know we became awful friendly and the first toim we stopped, when oi was walking her home, oi remember as clear as terday we squashed some elder and oi never smell that now without thinking o' that gal – as she was then. Well! Oi s'pose she was a couple o' years older'n me but we got on real well together. Allus ended up dancing together and then oi'd walk her home and things. Beautiful gal she was!

◇◇◇

I was absolutely amazed at this tale! Eventually I plucked up courage to ask his daughters – my cousins – if they had any inkling about this and both said that they had absolutely none – but I gained the impression that they were not exactly surprised that he had a 'liking for the ladies' when younger. I am absolutely sure that he was something of a 'romeo' in that early period of his young life from many of the things he said to me – hence the title of this book. He would laugh when I made comment about his behaviour as a 'young buck' but never made any attempt to deny it and, having admitted to some of the experiences of his youth would always end up by uttering his usual saying *'Yer don't want ter tek n' notice o' me – oim just a silly old bugger'.*

137

My Auntie Beat had been Nanny to the Bardwell family – who mainly lived in Scotland – so she rarely got home to her family in the neighbouring village of Great Yeldham. Then the Bardwells suffered terrible tragedies – one of their children was lost in the so-called 'Bermuda Triangle' – one of a number of apparently unexplained losses which occurred in that part of the Caribbean particularly in the 1920s and '30s. This had a devastating effect on the mother of the children who went on to commit suicide and so Beat returned home to soon find a similar post in Ridgewell to become Nanny to the Rose family who lived in a grand house there (this is the family still famed for the lime juices and preserves that carry the family name).

Now Beat was working in the same village where George worked and lived and they obviously met up and were then married immediately after Christmas (on 27th December) in 1930. Neither talked of their courtship or their wedding to me but George was then 31 and Beat 27.

George did explain how they came to move to Copford about 30 miles away. In those days almost all agricultural workers lived in what were called 'tied houses'. That meant that if the employee left the job he had to vacate the house – the house was 'tied' to the job. There being no such houses available in or around their villages – and there was a terrible world economic depression causing much unemployment – they had to look hard to find a job that offered a house with it. Thus they moved to new employers so that they could have a house and eventually moved once more to the cottage, that I recall so vividly, where they stayed until the end of their lives.

Between moving to 'the other soid o' Colchester' and my first memories of him and his family which I have recounted in earlier Chapters – George and Beat went about their business of working accomplished by hand, there is still a fair amount of 'hard grind' to be got through.

The first farm that George worked on after his marriage meant that he was required to look after a team of horses (he was a 'waggoner') and this, in turn, meant that he started even earlier in the morning than most of his workmates so that the horses were fed, cleaned out and re-bedded and groomed ready for when everyone else started work – horses being the motive power around the farm then.

All moving of goods (carting) was done by horses using either two or four-wheeled carts (the latter pulled by at least a pair of horses depending on the loads to be moved). All cultivations were similarly arranged and harvesting, too, was horse-powered. This also meant that to get any of the loads onto and off the carts was done by hand. So every farm employed quite large numbers of men. Today an all-arable farm might have one man/thousand acres. Up to the 1980s this would have been declining but pre-World War Two farms were not only much smaller but were heavily staffed – I reckon one man/25 acres might not be too far off the staffing rate without a livestock enterprise – and this would have then risen according to the type and number of animals kept. After all not crops all would be 'handled' but all ditches would be dug and cleaned by hand and hedges similarly trimmed. Hand-work was carried out all the year round.

Before World War Two broke out George and Beat moved to their final home where George was not only responsible for the horses but became the handy type of chap I have attempted to describe – the bloke who thatched the stacks of corn and beans to keep out the weather until these were thrashed during the winter and who made and repaired things.

139

from farm-to-farm. This equipment would have been pulled by the machine which then provided the motive power for the thrashing process which would have either been steam or a tractor. This equipment was set up so that the thrashing drum was close to the stack or positioned so that an elevator could be used to move the sheaves up onto the thrashing drum. All the necessary equipment (drum, baler) was driven by canvas belts from a flywheel on the steam engine/tractor. Sheaves were fed to the man stood on the drum who cut the strings of the sheaves and allowed them to peel gently into the top of the rotating drum which then separated grain, chaff and straw. The grain was bagged up, winched up using a hand-wound lift and then carried across a worker's shoulders to the barn for storage and use. The chaff would be bagged, carried into the end of the stable and tipped into a heap and fed to the horses (and, sometimes, beef cattle) over coming months. The straw would fall into the baler and be tied with wire into large half-ton plus monster bales. Clearly the man who dictated the speed of this process was the man who fed the sheaves into the drum – and that, invariably, was George.

Many years later, as a student, I was to be part of a team using this system for the thrashing of grass seed – although it is almost all harvested by combine harvesters now. What I recalled from watching George was that, without any evident effort, he cut all the strings from the sheaves at the point where it was knotted and skeins of these neatly cut strings were to be found in the barn where they could be later used to tie up sacks, etc. Do you know I found it very difficult – and far too slow -to locate the knots on the sheaves to do as George did without apparent effort! I remember my Auntie Beat telling me that, during those periods even when asleep!

At harvest time he would lead the team in the stackyard and would empty the carts thus dictating the speed at which the stacker and his mate worked. The others were all of a similar age to George but seemed to be content to defer to his setting of the pace and his ability to organise the tasks.

During World War Two the first tractors started to be more widely used and a number were imported from the USA while the infant UK tractor industry began to be established. George was never to become a tractor driver – he remained one of those who 'did things by hand'. That simply would not be possible today where arable workers have to be skilled operatives using extremely sophisticated machines and tractors which, individually, cost as much as a 100 acre farm would have cost 60 years ago. George was of that era – never complaining about the sheer 'slog' necessary in each season or the amount of lifting, throwing or carrying that was required. It is worth mentioning that all grain was then moved in sacks rather than in bulk as today. Wheat was in 2¼ cwt sacks (114kg), barley in 2 cwt sacks (102kg) and oats in 1¾ cwt (89kg) – all of which were carried across the shoulders of men on farms – no wonder that George was slightly round shouldered in old age!

When work was done he was an accomplished vegetable gardener – Auntie Beat tended to look after the flowers – and would have worked a garden of about ¼ acre – so no slacking when not at work!

Hobbies I saw little indication of – I have described that he was the local barber and used his shotgun to good effect to keep meat on the family table but he rarely went to the pub until he retired (his daughters probably think he made up for lost time

In World War Two he joined the Home Guard and he did tell me that *'things looked a bit nasty at one toim then Hitler took orff ter Russia instead'*. He did mention to me that they used to be on night training and guarding places and I asked him, when a boy, 'Did you have the next day off work then?' to which he snorted *'Blast no! Yer just got on wi' things – no toim ter be orff work'*. His experience of being in World War One meant that George had some responsibility in his local Home Guard unit – which also explains why those who worked on the farm with him tended to defer to him in terms of how team tasks were organised as most would have been in the Home Guard with him too.

'Just got on with things' is another expression firmly attached to my memories of George. I accept that we now live in different times but his willingness to accept things – even when not pleasant or remotely enjoyable – 'as they are' and to simply carry on are a real part of his character. I guess we will never know if that was always a part of how he looked at life or whether his Wartime experiences and working in a tough industry conditioned him to be that way. I feel pretty sure that my generation – and even more so those behind me – would simply not 'put up with' some of the things that George's generation did. Trying to understand whether the George that I knew and loved was always a stoical sort of bloke or whether he became so as a result of what he had to face is something I bet that he never analysed for himself. He just left the likes of me wondering!

Although there is absolutely no chance that George continued his 'love of the ladies' into his married life it would be remiss of me to – as well as being inaccurate – to cover up George's penchant for female company when a young and single man but

When I had been 'pulling his leg' about his days as a young 'gadabout' in the 1920s he laughed a lot and accepted the banter but as it died down he turned to me and said with total conviction: *'Corse all that there foolin' around stopped when oi got meself fixed up with yer Auntie Beat, y'know.'*

I could tell that that was the reality of his life from then on – it was, clearly, the truth. It remained so all his days – he had no time at all for *'them silly devils who mess family loif up boi chasing a bit o' skirt'*. As he aged and mellowed, and I got to know the 'real him' better – indeed, as I got older and was able to discern such things – he became a real champion of the role of women in life. He thought that they had the 'rough end of life's stick' being left to cope with the mundane bits of life while we blokes could get out of the house when the children were ill or fractious and when routine tasks needing attending to. He thought that men had the better end of the whole 'deal' because at least we could get out to see our workmates and get on with our jobs to take our minds of the inconveniences of life.

This was perfectly illustrated for me by the way he treated my wife when he stayed with us. When I got grumpy – all too frequently, of course – he would always take her side and tell me *'Cor y'don't know how lucky y'are, boi – she's a luvly gal'*. The fact that he was right wasn't the point – he felt that we blokes had the better part of life and should behave with proper consideration of our partners. That has always helped prove, in my mind, that all his 'gallavanting' – as he might well have called it – ceased when he got engaged to my Auntie Beat.

So that just about rounds his story up – I started this from when I first knew him and have tried to link that with this school, army and working life to form a picture of the lovely did nothing out o' the ordinary. I, of course, beg to disagree with his assessment.

CHAPTER SEVENTEEN

◇◇

George got over his first stroke – which, as explained, he was always in denial about – but simply got older. His two daughters were mindful of that and both were wonderful in the way that they cared for him. His granddaughters always did their part in that process too. They all made sure that he was well fed, had clean clothes (even if any new shirt they bought him soon had burn marks in it from his cigarettes!) and, although they chided him about it, made sure that the house was clean. Just as important to him – it seemed at times – they ensured that his three+ bottles of whisky per week were always available!

He continued to make his runner bean wine to go with it and life went on that way until the late autumn of 1997 when he had 'the big one'.

My sister rang us to tell us that George's eldest daughter had called her to say that he was in hospital having had a really speak.

My wife and I plucked up the courage to go and see him before Christmas and found him in a beautifully situated converted mansion in a pleasant large room. He recognised us in an instant and was very animated as we recounted our life and news to him – but he could not speak and it clearly made him very cross that he couldn't do so. His brain was working fine but his voicebox wasn't responding as he wanted it to.

It was very hard work talking to him as I had to try to guess what he wanted to know – he got everything from the news about our home and sons, our garden, my career, politics, football and cricket and the great storm which had brought thousands of trees down around the country – and in the grounds of the nursing home too, I recall. He was obviously frustrated that he could not converse with us. When his youngest daughter arrived she took my wife away for a chat and left us alone and I remember making a special effort to talk to him like I used to when we were having a drink together.

So, I told him that he was a 'bad old bugger who drank too much, had broken too many hearts when he was younger and who caused mischief when in one of his cussed moods'. It was a somewhat half-hearted bit of ribbing but he enjoyed the banter – as he always did – he threw his head back and smiled (he wasn't able to laugh) while I was teasing him.

I felt extremely sad though and must admit that I found it very difficult to keep this up. George would not have expected me to give him a hug – although I wish I had – but I did take a firm grip on his arm when I found it too difficult to keep the conversation going. My way of assuring him how much I loved him – George, himself, was anything BUT tactile.

that was what we expected we did not care for the prognosis.

Then Gill produced a small bottle of whisky and poured some into his glass at the side of his bed. She held the glass so that he could drink it. He had several like this – he drank enough to have made me absolutely sozzled over the next hour I admit.

That was how we left him – a part-paralysed 89-year-old who had just enjoyed his favourite tipple – but who could neither say nor wave goodbye to us.

That was the final time that we saw him. He died in February 1998 and took the rest of his wartime and lifetime memories with him untold.

My poor wife, terribly upset herself, saw me more emotionally upset and uncontrolled at his funeral than I can recall being at any other point in our lives together. I have felt somewhat embarrassed on occasions that, when my father died some three and a half years later, I was able to remain dry-eyed and emotionally in control managing even to read one of the lessons. Yet, I could not have done so at George's funeral.

I had become much closer to George as a man and a mate than I ever got to my father as an adult – even though I was close to my Dad as a boy and I never, ever had a cross word with him. I felt George's passing terribly and can recall little of the day of his funeral other than standing in the churchyard after the service with my whole body wracked with grief at his passing.

I still feel that same sadness for his absence from my life today.

It is amazing to me how often that I still think about him. Friends and acquaintances have had to suffer me telling them about the man and his exploits many times over the years. He would be astonished that his experiences – told only to me, it now appears, have been passed on to others as he always said

147

While that may have been true – and it is the case that he spent much less time at the front than many, many others – few could have bottled those experiences up for so long and then let some of them out in such an innocent and unexpected way.

Why he told me, and no one else about these things, we will never know. The sad and ironical thing is that he may well have spoken more about things to those with whom he served in Flanders and France – but many of those did not survive to share those experiences with others. So these stories remained unrecounted until George sat down with me late in his days and we shared a drink – and he smoked his fags.

His son-in-law reckons that I became 'the son that he never had' and that he loved yarning over a drink with someone especially after he had to live on his own when Beat died. There may be some substance to that but whatever the reason I am honoured that he chose me to talk to and left an impact on my character greater than anyone else that I can think of.

He made me interested in the realities of World War One – I have read countless words about it since. I have visited some of the sites that the British Army fought over in and before 1918 and to try and follow in his footsteps in Belgium and France. In addition I have made pilgrimages to countless museums that deal with the subject both to learn more and to honour those who were involved in that terrible war. I live in total awe of those who survived such horrors and nightmares and who, like George, managed to live apparently 'normal' lives thereafter with such experiences and secrets locked away inside them. I feel sure that I have been emotionally 'scarred' by matters of much less consequence – and for much less reason – than they had and have been a poorer member of society than most of them. Yet George bringing a more lasting peace across western Europe possible – some 27 years later.

Somewhat perversely one of my favourite films is *Oh! What A Lovely War* which heavily parodied the events and characters involved in World War One. I have always loved irreverence I am afraid and enjoyed the fun it poked at 'The Blimps' or public school educated officers. I didn't dare tell George that I enjoyed it though as I would never have wanted him to know that I found that time, so terrible to those that were there, amusing in any way. Probably though, knowing him at that stage of his life, he might well have laughed too. I never put it to the test though.

I feel sure that great world events define the lives of those who live through them. George's life was defined by World War One and fashioned by the experiences he had lived through at that time. Even those who are non-participants are affected by such huge factors like war – because I have made sure that I have explained it to them – I am sure that my grandchildren realise that my character was as much shaped by my living through World War Two and the austere years that followed it as it was by the trauma of the early death of my mother when I was still young.

George and others have often attempted to explain the excitement and optimism – hugely misplaced of course – that was felt by most of the population when the so-called Great War was declared. Patriotism was pronounced too and because the British had 'guaranteed Belgian neutrality' once the Germans moved into Belgium we were deemed to have right on our side and to have just cause to declare war on Germany. In fact over one million men had volunteered by the end of 1914 – many in the so-called 'Pals Battalions' when groups of men from a given locality joined

149

hated the Germans. Once he had been in the front line though any hatred that he might have felt melted away into mutual sympathy for the enemy – at least those who were in a similar position to himself.

It is interesting to reflect on the fact when World War Two was declared, despite the horrors of the First being very fresh in everyone's minds, there was little outcry against fighting so again soon. The population was more pragmatic and realistic about the need to fight again and about how long it would take to deal with the problem facing our society and about the terrible deadly nature of war. I honestly feel that the brave and stoical manner in which those who had fought in World War One conducted themselves, their reluctance to talk about it, in the main, and the manner in which they shrugged off the effects of their experiences upon them made it easier for the next generation to accept the call to arms for the second time in a lifetime. Certainly I never heard George condemn our politicians for making that decision to mobilise yet again.

CHAPTER EIGHTEEN

◇◇◇

Nine million people died during World War One – the biggest proportion perished as a result of murderous shellfire. There were 46 million casualties. As if to make it certain that the 20th century would be a quite dreadful one – many millions more people around the world died of the influenza virus (H1 – similar to the so called 'swine flu' epidemic in the early 21st century). The effects of the, so called, 'Spanish influenza' rumbled on around the world from 1918 until the mid-1920s.

On Monday 11th November 1918 the then British Prime Minister David Lloyd George stood up in Parliament and said:

'At 11 o'clock this morning came to an end the cruellest and most terrible war that has ever scourged mankind. I hope that we may say that thus, this fateful morning, came to an end all wars'.

but produce the substrate in which the seeds of a second world war could flourish and grow towards its ultimate 'flowering' in 1939 when Germany again 'took on the world'.

Everyone in the world became affected by World War One – as they were by the Second just 20 years later. The second time around there was little of the sense of adventure that George said many who volunteered for the first war felt at the outset. He said once *'Ter start with everyone seemed excoited and pleased to join up'* – second time around most waited until conscripted to fight and there was much less expectation that volunteers would come forward.

Debate about the conduct of World War One continues to this day. Whether one believes Allied generals to be 'butchers and fools' or just men who were dealt an 'un-winnable hand' is very much a matter of informed, personal opinion. George missed all the early horrors which originated in poor tactics and un-preparedness for the industrial-scale carnage that modern weapons could wreak. Perhaps many of the unsatisfactory outcomes of Allied offences stemmed from an over-aggressive policy and poor coordination associated with unsatisfactory intelligence of the obstacles facing them. This policy of assault gave rise to our soldiers having poorer trenches and defences than those planned-in by the Germans – the British considered trenches as 'starting off points for the next 'big push' while the Germans were more pragmatic and heavily reinforced their defensive positions making them easier to defend and it was only when the Allies coordinated their attacks with artillery, air support and tanks and became better-prepared to resist counter-attacks that they made real progress – even then to achieve all objectives within the planned time scale was rare even in 1918.

Made Em Cry.indd 152

11/8/2012 1:40:08

some 25 miles north of Paris. Much of 1915 and the first half of 1916 was concerned with attritional fighting with little movement by either side and gradually Britain and its Commonwealth allies assumed responsibility for larger parts of the front due to the heavy losses suffered by the French. By the time that the first major British offensive was launched in Picardy (The Somme) in July 1916 most of the experienced professional soldiers were dead or wounded. The Germans recovered most of the gains made during that offensive and much of the next set of advances achieved following the huge Allied offensive the following year resulted from a planned withdrawal by the Germans to their heavily fortified lines in Picardy (The Hindenburg Line) – see map on pages 98 and 99. It was from these well-prepared positions that the Germans made their final charge for Paris and the Channel ports in the spring and early summer of 1918 which, as earlier described earlier, this was halted around the time that George and his contemporaries (who had initially been held back in England) were released by Lloyd George, the Prime Minister, to help stem the advance.

The end came relatively swiftly as hunger and exhaustion overcame the Germans and the home support for the war in Germany itself began to crumble and starvation took its toll on the home front as well.

The position in which Germany then found itself saw their Monarchy disappear and the country become a Republic. The upheavals that followed that major change gave rise to the growth of National Socialism with the Nazi party taking power. This saw, during the 1930s, a more aggressive and newly-confident Germany appear which felt more sure of its place in the world. A country that had largely side-stepped the effects of the

War Two was hoving into view.

This reflection on those times through some of the experiences of the life of George Ellis brings world affairs into focus through an ordinary – yet extraordinary – man. I have never seen – neither would I be capable of composing – any words that summarise how I feel about George, and men like him, that are more appropriate than those that formed part of a speech by the then-Prime Minister of Australia, Paul Keating MP. He delivered these words at the burial of the Unknown Australian soldier who, after services honouring him in France, was flown home to be buried in his home land on Armistice Day (11th November 1993). Mr Keating's speech is enscribed on the Commonwealth Graves Memorial near the River Somme where so many Australians died and are buried alongside British and other Allied soldiers. It reads:

Because the Great War was a mad, brutal, awful struggle distinguished more often than not by military and political incompetence; because the waste of human life was so terrible that some said that victory was scarcely discernable from defeat; and because the war which was supposed to end all wars in fact sowed the seeds of a second, even more terrible war – we might think that the Unknown Soldier died in vain.

But in honouring our war dead, as we always have, we declare that this is not true.

For out of war came a lesson which transcended the horror and tragedy and the inexcusable folly.

It was a lesson about ordinary people – that lesson was that they were _not_ ordinary.

That could have been written for and about George as far as I am concerned – despite his protestations to the contrary, his

Made Em Cry.indd   154

11/8/2012   1:40:08

that he did proved that he was one of those 'not ordinary' of men. Thank God for him and those like him who formed the basis of our society today.

156

157

159

ND - #0321 - 270225 - C0 - 234/156/10 - PB - 9781780910642 - Gloss Lamination